THE PSYCHIC IS YOU

THE PSYCHIC IS YOU

How to Develop
Your Own Psychic Ability

Kathlyn Rhea
with Maggie O'Leary

Celestial Arts
Millbrae, California

Cover design: Abigail Johnston
Cover photograph and lab work: George Post

Celestial Arts
231 Adrian Road
Millbrae, California 94030

First Printing, September 1979

Made in the United States of America

Library of Congress Cataloging in Publication Data

Rhea, Kathlyn.
    The psychic.

    1.   Psychical research.   2.   Rhea, Kathlyn.   I.   Title.
BF1031.R366   133.8′092′4   [B]   79-53023
ISBN 0-89087-194-9

1   2   3   4   5   6   7   8 — 86   85   84   83   82   81   80   79

Contents

Foreword

This book is the road to my own psychic. It took years of diligence and delight to live it, to overcome the fear of the unknown, and the need to mysticize what I now regard as a natural extension of our sensory heritage.

While I do not profess to have all the answers, I believe I've discovered some interesting ones. If any of them serve as tools for your own search, then I will have succeeded in showing that the psychic is indeed you.

Kathlyn Rhea

Acknowledgments

Heading the list of those I wish to acknowledge is my daughter, Cynthia, who was the first to spend innumerable days organizing my notes, pouring effort and understanding into the birth of my thoughts, and for creating the illustrations that accompany this book.

There are also others without whom the long task of completing this book would have seemed insurmountable. They encouraged me when the going was difficult, assisted when finances were low, and always provided the warmth and friendship and faith when I needed it most: Donna and Dale Pedersen; Dr. Benjamin Ichinose; Tom Mathews; Carolyn and Alvy Moore; Lucy MacDougall; Paul Unruh; Ronnie Hall; Judy and Rick von Schlegell; Joyce Coit; and to Jeffrey Furst. To Katrina and Yiwen Tang, M.D., and Sandy and Bert Rettner, M.D., my loving gratitude for nurturing me through a fractured back during the writing of this book.

My heartfelt thanks to Maggie O'Leary and Judy Nichols, two very talented ladies who carried the manuscript to completion by spending additional hours putting the last pages into place and editing the completed manuscript, none of which would have been of value without the outstanding staff at Celestial Arts, whose enthusiasm and visionary spirits made this book a reality. And to the teachers I met along the way in my quest for what Psychic really meant, I would like to extend my deepest appreciation for the knowledge they shared.

Dedication

This book is dedicated to four people with whom sharing this life has been an exciting, loving and learning experience: my daughter, Cynthia Rink Allan, and my sons William, Christopher and Charles Rink. They have given me love and understanding while I plunged into this uncharted world of ESP, and accepted the role it played in their daily lives as well as mine. I have marveled as I have watched them achieve a beautiful blend of intelligence and intuition.

ONE
Everyone Is Psychic

Has anyone ever told you that they believe you are psychic? Did it intrigue you, make you feel that you had been singled out, that you were special? Well, you *are* special—unique, in fact—but not because of your psychic sensitivity. Every human being is psychic!

"I was just thinking of you," you marvel when a childhood friend phones to say she's just arrived at the local airport.

"I knew this was going to happen," you grumble as you jack up the car to fix a flat and resign yourself to missing the opening curtain.

"I knew I shouldn't have done that," you say ruefully, looking back on the ruins of a love affair rushed into despite a "feeling" that the partner wasn't really right for you.

"Something tells me I should stay out of this," you murmur to yourself, and this time you quietly exit as your mother and your lover start to "discuss" women's lib.

The minute your daughter walks through the door you know something is troubling her. You answer the phone before it rings. You have a disturbing dream about someone, and later hear that the person was in extreme danger at that moment. You have a dream in which you are visited by a person who has just died. You suddenly see, in your imagination, a strange face, and a week later you meet that person at a party.

All of us function on this intuitive level all the time, but we rarely notice that we are doing so. *That is because it is so natural.*

The flow of consciousness is ever-present. Some people call it "God," some call it "universal consciousness," still others call it "mind." We are all part of it, whether we are aware of it or not.

We enter the psychic realm when we heighten our perception of consciousness. Because we become more aware, it is often spoken of as a state of "higher" consciousness. It is a sense of knowing before you can put words or actions to something, and it involves the use of all our physical senses: taste, touch, hearing, sight and smell. You might think of the five senses as various musical notes and the psychic sense as a chord that integrates them all.

I like to think of higher consciousness as an immense lake. We may have our backs turned and be unaware of it, but that doesn't mean it ceases to exist. We can sit and contemplate it from afar. We can walk to the lake shore and step into it. We can wade in it up to our ankles, our knees, or our waists. Perhaps we will choose to swim in it, and we can do so to whatever depth and breadth we desire. The lake is there, offering us many possibilities. It is up to us.

Most people protest that they are not psychic. I believe it is simply that they have never taken the time to explore that aspect of themselves. Probably they have been influenced by the prevailing notion that psychic sensitivity is a "gift," a fragile thing mysteriously visited upon only a few people. Nonsense!

I can pick up the telephone right now and dial a number to get the time and temperature. All I have to do is make the effort and I will receive the information. People who say they are not psychic are not picking up their telephones.

When someone tells me how fortunate I am to be so "gifted," it makes me laugh. Gifts are free. I worked very hard to develop my psychic sense. It all comes down to training, training, training. I spent many hours exploring the world about me as well as looking within myself to reach this level of awareness. I was, indeed, "fortunate"—fortunate to have many well-educated, intelligent friends, including psychiatrists, GPs, diplomats and teachers, who were willing to knock ideas around and share their feelings about life. They were precious channels available to me.

The point is—and there is nothing more important in this entire book—that you and everyone else can do the same thing if you are willing to practice. You must be willing to go swimming in the lake of consciousness.

I am frequently asked if some people are simply better at it than others. This is true to some extent. In the same way, some people are natural artists. They have such a talent for what they do that they can produce beautiful work with ease. But everyone can learn to draw something; it's just that, for some people to be artists, they must really work at it. No one would expect to paint masterpieces after a few days' study.

Everyone has some degree of psychic rapport with family and friends, and has experienced incidents such as those at the beginning of the chapter. This rapport is often greatly enhanced between twins. I know of twin boys who, because they were so completely on each others' wavelengths, were placed in separate classrooms at school. One morning one of the twins dropped his pencil on the floor under his desk. When he bent down to retrieve it, he cracked his head on the desk with enough force that he was slightly stunned. He was still slumped groggily under his desk when his twin, down the hall in another classroom, got up, walked out of the room, down the hall and into the other room, where he crawled under the desk to see if his brother was OK.

A woman I counseled as an adult told me that in her pre-school years she had a playmate who was invisible to everyone else in the family. The little girl described her friend and told the family her name. The parents became sufficiently concerned that they took their daughter to a doctor, who assured them that she merely had a vivid imagination. On the first day of school, my client walked into her class, looked at a little girl across the room and ran over to hug her. The children called each other by name. When the teacher asked how long the girls had known each other and heard the strange facts, she called their parents. It seemed both children had, prior to school, played with an imaginary playmate. Each had been described and named as the other.

These things happen too frequently to be labeled mere coincidence. They are examples of people who are swimming in the lake of consciousness. They have investigated the personal part of the lake.

Some of our great inventors seemed merely to sit down and have world-changing ideas come to them. They weren't such unusual people; they simply took the time to contemplate a certain part of the lake and then plunged in, absorbing everything in the way of relevant knowledge. I don't believe there is anything that is not already in that lake, waiting for the right person. If you're in electronics, or medicine, or teaching, you can go to your sector of the lake and immerse yourself in knowledge. With practice you can focus on what you need, and it will be yours.

People like me, who train day after day, are going to venture further than the boundaries of our immediate families and careers. We are going to enter the worlds of total strangers (with their permission, of course) and very soon will move out into the universe. Indeed, this has happened already.

Ingo Swann is a psychic who does so-called astral or out-of-body travel. Under a controlled experiment by a research institute, and physically separated by fifteen hundred miles, Swann and another well-known psychic, Harold Sherman, "traveled" to the planet Jupiter. Separately they took notes, which were put into a vault unopened until a U.S. government space probe reached Jupiter and sent its information back.

The results were startling. When Swann's and Sherman's notes were opened and compared with the information from the space probe, they were found to be almost identical. They even contained the same surprises for scientists concerning hitherto unknown facts about the atmosphere of that planet. Those two men had obviously dipped into the interplanetary sector of the lake.

There are specific sectors that I enjoy, such as those to do with education and medicine and criminology. But I probably won't get into those parts to do with engineering, for instance, because that isn't relevant to my life. However, if an engineer came to me for counseling, I would be able to tap that area, to bring forth information for him. I may not use it, but it is still there if I need it. To be psychic is to allow the lake of consciousness to flow around and through you. The professional psychic not only allows it to do so, but goes out to seek it.

There are many psychics, some well-known, who tell me that when God hits them with a lightning bolt, they get a psychic flash. They say, "I can't do it on my own; God does it for me." Well, I believe that "God helps those who help themselves." The inner self, or higher consciousness, helps the outer self if one is willing to use it. I reject the idea that we are helpless pawns. Essentially, these lightning-bolt psychics are saying that consciousness controls us. I simply don't believe that. It is irresponsible.

If you come to me and ask me how a trip is going to turn out, I can deliberately take you into the future, put you aboard the plane, see how you look, how you feel, who is around you, and how they feel. I then take you off the plane, see who meets you, and what happens. Then I put you back on a plane, and fly you home safe and sound, even though none of it has happened in everyday time. But I am in complete control of what I am seeing and feeling, and my answers to you will be a product of controlled accuracy. If I have to wait until a bolt comes out of the blue, I'm not going to be much good to you when you need a fast answer!

This may raise the question of time. How do I see past, present and future? Time is man-made, a way we have chosen to organize our perceptions of the world. Think of an astronaut, thousands of miles out in space, who can see the entire earth at once. If he were to look at the Amazon River, for instance, he could see its entire length and all its tributaries. As he neared earth, though, his view would progressively narrow, until, if he were to splash down in the river, he would be conscious of only a very small part of it. He would be blinded by the Now, as we all are to some extent. But past, present and future exist simultaneously and can be looked into with equal ease by those who train themselves as I have.

Especially when you become aware of the psychic realm you realize that, in dreams and in memory, past and future are there, ready to be tapped at will. Just recall a time when you have unexpectedly smelled a certain fragrance and that scent has transported you all but physically to a certain incident in your past. Some people experience this more acutely with music.

Most of us have had an experience that the French call *déjà vu*. Meaning "seen before," the term refers to the feeling that you have already had in the past the experience that you are having in the present. In the midst of conversation you will suddenly feel that you have said the same words, heard the same responses, before. You will "recall" the entire incident precisely as it is now occurring. Usually this sense is so delicate, so fleeting, that when you try to take control of it with your mind, it vanishes. There is a theory that the sense of *déjà vu* is actually the experience in your mind of something *before* it happens.

Past, present and future all flow together. It can flow through me, if I wish. It doesn't just happen in unexpected moments. It is there all the time, and at the same time. But *we* have to decide what and when to draw from it. We have to control it, too. And every one of us can do that if we are willing to try.

TWO
Training Myself As A Psychic

As a young woman, my mother was able to bring the fragrance of flowers into a room so strongly that those present could identify the particular flower she had in mind. People told her it was evil to do that. Perhaps that is one reason she found it so difficult to deal with me when I was a child. Even at the age of two, I remember that there were all these things going on in my world that weren't necessarily in my room, yet I knew them.

You may have a child say to you that there is "something" in the closet or under the bed, and your first impulse is to reassure. "It's all right, there's nothing there," you say soothingly. The child may not be afraid at all, but nevertheless is quite certain there *is* something in the closet. However, the lesson is quickly learned that one cannot talk about "things" in the closet.

When I was a young child I was terrified of the dark, because I was aware of things happening in the room. I would sense the unseen presence of people, and of course I kept both parents up night after night. They would show me there was no one under the bed, in the closet, and so on, and naturally were much annoyed at having their sleep disturbed by my fears. Because there was never an explanation of what I was experiencing, I carried my terror into adulthood. As a grown, married woman I had to leave the lights on when my husband was away at sea. It literally caused me pain to be alone at night. Only after I began exploring psychic phenomena did I find release from the fear. I realized that it is very natural to be more receptive and aware at night, and finally the pains went away.

I was very young when I realized that adults don't always tell the truth. I could tell when they were lying, but I soon discovered that pointing out the lies invariably led to a spanking. My knowledge made life very difficult for me and for my mother, who wanted me to accept the world as everyone else did.

My father was a man of few words, but he was a Pied Piper to people and to animals. He must have had excellent ESP, because he always seemed to *know*. I didn't have to explain things to Dad.

I began to realize I was "aware" very early. I could see the discrepancies between the way adults said the world was, and the way it actually was. Mother was thrown into confusion by my certainty, which she interpreted as rebelliousness. "Why are you always going against what I say?" she would ask. "As long as I know it is right, I don't care what others say." This was not a popular attitude coming from a young child. Mother was trying to follow the book and I was trying to throw it away.

Teachers and other adults attributed my special ability to pick up knowledge to an extra-vivid imagination. Nevertheless, when I started to school I was immediately skipped forward a grade. It has been said that Edgar Cayce could put a book under his pillow and know the contents the next morning. Without putting anything under my pillow, I must have absorbed things in much the same way.

When I was about nine, I was sitting on the front porch

steps in the warm sunshine, puzzling over the idea that God had somehow created all this world around me out of nothing. How could that be? Suddenly there was this complete awareness, quite beyond that of a child, an awareness of the soul so profound that I can still recall it clearly. I was conscious of the little girl acting out the role of Kay Rhea, but I could also see myself as a total person who could detach and look at that surface part of me. It was exciting to see myself as my mother and others did, and a little scary at first.

Every so often, after that day, I would go back to that state. I realize now that I was meditating. The very word *meditation* has taken on a portentous tone, so that we often forget what a simple thing it really is, and how naturally accessible to all.

Because of my early experiences, I am always mindful of the highly intuitive nature of children. Newborn babies are like psychic sponges, eagerly absorbing everything around them as they come to know the world. This awareness usually dissipates throughout childhood as adults firmly impose the limitations of the physical world upon them. But there is much to be learned if we really listen to what children tell us.

In a recent case, a boy was stolen by his father after a bitter court battle in which total custody was awarded to the mother. I asked her whether the boy had said anything that presaged the kidnapping. She suddenly realized that her son had warned her. He had become reluctant to go to school, and when she asked why, he said he was afraid his daddy would take him away from her. Although she feared that very thing, the mother assured the boy it wouldn't happen. He was kidnapped a few days later. If the woman had come to me beforehand, I could have attested to the child's reliability and helped her to recognize her own anxiety and take protective measures.

In a more tragic case, a child was abducted and killed. A few days before the event, he had started to ask his mother if he was going to die. Because his mother didn't feel like dealing with questions of life and death just then, she avoided talking to him about it. A few days afterward he was murdered.

In my seminars and lectures I always encourage my audience to learn to listen to their children. A police officer who attended my seminar recently told me of the radical change in his relationship with his two-year-old since he started really tuning in to the child. The results can be amazing.

If my insights created problems for me as a child, they became even more burdensome when I was a teenager. Everyone likes to get compliments, but I could always tell when a boy was handing me a line. I would know in advance if a date was going to be late, and it would make me irritable because I hated waiting. If a boy broke a date for a good reason, I could accept that, but I always knew if he was lying. In high school I was madly in love with a handsome, blond Swede who was a number of years older than I. Though his behavior seemed faithful and sincere, and he had told my parents he wanted to marry me after we finished college, I kept seeing something in those beautiful blue eyes that made me uncomfortable. Sure enough, it came out that he was also seeing an "older" woman, and I felt quite heartbroken for a while. Sometimes that kind of knowing isn't much fun.

I entered college at fifteen, but found it terribly boring because I already "knew" what I was studying. It seemed silly that I should be required to write the information for the professor. To this day I hate to write anything because my thoughts come faster than I can get them down.

It was at fifteen, too, that I started to model. My brother carried my picture with him when he went in the service, and a man who was a magazine illustrator saw it and asked if he could get in touch with me. He invited me to model for women's magazines, and I continued modeling even after my marriage.

I often think the real reason I married my first husband was that it was a necessary part of my destiny to meet his father, who was a physician. My father-in-law was the first person who ever talked to me about psychic phenomena. He spoke of making diagnoses strictly from a psychic level that proved to be accurate upon physical examination. At that time he felt he could not discuss the psychic with patients or with many other people, but he would talk to me for hours because I saw nothing odd about it.

He was very scholarly, and highly developed as a psychic. He had predicted that my husband would become a military aviator when he was still a child, and I think he saw that one day I would be very involved in psychic realms. He told me that he was studying with numerous people, but on the psychic plane, not the everyday one. "I even study with some you would think of as dead," he added.

One evening he said to me, "My most recent lesson is an interesting one. My teacher sent me a bouquet of flowers. I am to find the scientific explanation as to how this can happen." He then explained to me that the flowers were *apports*, objects transported psychically into the physical plane. I was in awe of these things, but they felt perfectly natural to me.

I anticipated our meetings eagerly, and read every new book on psychic phenomena. The doctor was my first real teacher on the subject, though I only listened and made no attempt to act on the knowledge at that time.

When my children started arriving, I opened my first modeling and charm school in Virginia, where we were then stationed. I was told that many people had earlier tried to open modeling agencies in that town, but none succeeded. My success may have signaled the first application of my psychic abilities, though I wasn't aware of it at the time. Many times I have known something would be successful, though others told me it was impossible. Sometimes I have followed my hunch, others not. But when I have paid attention to my intuition, I have been right.

Every place we were stationed I would establish my own modeling school and agency. In addition, I often had television and radio shows and would help with local segments of state and national beauty contests and fashion shows. In those days we found ourselves stationed all over the world. I opened the first teenage modeling agency in Japan. Some of the American girls were so successful that the Japanese offered them big contracts to stay. All along, even at the peak of my business success, my reading and interest in ESP remained, although I had few friends with whom I could discuss it.

Eventually my husband was assigned to an aircraft carrier as Executive Officer. We lived in Florida during the two years of his command, and I saw him very seldom. Once again I had a modeling agency and a TV show. I had developed my fashion shows to the point where they included rock bands, ballet troupes, and choral groups. I felt that I had done as much as I wanted to do with that career. I became a serious student of psychic phenomena.

One of the first psychics I met was Bartie Butcher, a retired school teacher who used her sparkling blue eyes to look into a crystal ball. After several visits, I suspected it was not the crystal ball which produced the visions, but she insisted that I try to use it. I looked into that thing until my eyes crossed and my elbows ached, but I never saw anything.

I began going from psychic to psychic, asking questions, studying and meditating. I wanted to know how they could see things in people's palms, and why the tarot cards looked different each time when they were always the same cards. How did they *see* what they saw? They told me they didn't *want* to "know" what they knew, "see" what they saw—it just happened. Many gave me spiritual or religious answers of some sort. On many points they disagreed with each other. No one satisfied my curiosity.

In Jacksonville a lovely lady of mixed black and Indian heritage made a lasting impression on me. She was a counselor who flew each month to a neighboring state to advise a governor's wife. As I sat in her waiting room with three others, she appeared and looked us over. "I'll see you first," she said, pointing to me. Once we were alone she told me I was very psychic and would one day be doing what she was doing: counseling. Then she gave me some advice, which I still had to learn the hard way. She told me always to charge something for my services. Sometimes she charged just one rose if people could afford no more.

She asked me to do a reading for her. I was scared stiff— I'd never done one before. I told her that I saw her in a long gown, which I described. Many people were watching as she was handed some flowers while standing on a stage. When I finished, she said that I had described the dress she was planning to wear to her anniversary at her church, where it was likely that she would be presented with flowers. It was reassuring to get instant feedback on what I had seen. It was still an unusual occurrence.

My explorations in all directions contined. Joe Dickerson, a well-known trance medium, sometimes brought his wife and grandchildren to my house for dinner. Afterwards they would sit around the table and say what they were seeing. My daughter would see things, too, and she drew what she saw, as she is an artist. Everyone seemed to be seeing things but me.

Finally I decided that I needed my own accuracy check. In the Florida town where we lived, the dog races were listed each day in the local newspaper, along with the winners of the previous day. Here was the almost instant accuracy check I wanted. I proceeded to pick each day's winners, usually by just sitting down and seeing if I felt anything about each dog. I asked various psychics to pick the winners, too. Each day I would check to see how accurate I was, and if my psychic friends were accurate. I also made notes on how I came to choose each winner—whether I did it by reading cards, "seeing" the winner, or just having a feeling that a certain dog would win.

After my accuracy was high, I occasionally went to·the

tracks and placed some bets. One day I took the crystal-ball lady, Bartie, with me. As we sat in the clubhouse, she looked into her glass of beer, exclaimed "I see a five! I see a five!" and immediately left to place a bet. Away from her crystal she still thought she needed something to "see" into, if only a glass of beer. Her beer "crystal" was often right.

On another occasion, one of the professional gamblers who frequented the track had evidently been watching me cash in my winning tickets for the last several races. The next time I got up to place a bet, he edged over to glance at my racing form. I left him with a very puzzled look on his face. What baffled him was "saw moon, bet on Crescent Lady"; "large brown dog stops at corner building"; "number fourteen in crystal, twenty in cards, fifty-two in writing." I was trying everything from crystal balls to tarot cards to automatic writing to see just what worked, and how.

My attempts at automatic writing were frustrating. After a few weeks of waiting for the pencil to move, I said aloud, "All right, if this works, give me the four numbers for the Big Q at the race track." The Big Q is a bet on the last two races of the day. The next-to-the-last race, you buy tickets on one number to win and one number to place. If the dogs with those numbers win, you turn in your tickets and replace them with the numbers for the last race. If you pick all four numbers correctly, you win very big money.

So I sat there and four numbers appeared on the page, written in my handwriting with the pencil. I kept getting the same four numbers over and over, but because I had no previous success with automatic writing I was very skeptical. I think that the next day I checked the paper to see if those four numbers had won, but they had not.

Several weeks later, I went to the track again. It came time for the Big Q and I chose two numbers that felt right to me. They won. Then I had to choose the two numbers for the last race. I felt that I should know which two numbers to choose, but everyone was giving me advice. Finally I simply chose two numbers at random. They lost. Looking at the winning numbers on the board, I kept thinking "Those numbers look so familiar to me. Now where have I seen them?"

Driving home, they still bothered me. Then I remembered. "Oh, no! Those are the four numbers I wrote all afternoon a few weeks ago!" I was so annoyed with myself.

Some time later, Bartie Butcher looked into her crystal ball and told me "Kay, you are going to win the Big Q soon. There will be someone named Kelly at the track with you." When I got home that night my daughter said that a friend of the family, a naval aviator named Kelly, was in town. He wanted me to call him at his hotel. Having learned my psychic lesson, I telephoned "Hi, George. You have a date at the race track tonight." We went to the track and, sure enough, I won over three thousand dollars in the Big Q that night! You have to listen to *all* the messages.

I ran into a lot of disapproval from my psychic friends (other than Bartie) for betting on the dogs myself. They told me I would lose my psychic "powers" if I used them for personal gain. How I hate that inflated word! I don't believe that any more than I believe that their eyes would be taken from them for reading the racing forms.

My only piece of advice is this: Make your decisions before you go to the track. There you will pick up the confusion of other people. Pick the winners before you leave home and stick to them.

About the time I was seeing these psychics and having discussions and meditation groups with friends, my housekeeper, Ann, who was naturally psychic, complained to me that she "didn't mind all those people coming and doing what they do, but I sure hate them leaving their haunts behind." I asked what she meant by "their haunts." "Well, I hear somebody at the door and I go and nobody is there. I hear somebody walking down the hall and I look and no one is there. When you're not in the house, I carry around your big old cat to protect me." I tried to comfort her by telling her that "they" wouldn't hurt her, and she said "Yeah, but they're sure going to make me hurt myself!"

Often during that period of searching I felt like a failure. All around me people were seeing things and hearing things and I wasn't. Finally, after about six months of steady, day-to-day work, during most of which I was trying too hard to "see" with my conscious eyes, I began to have the psychic experiences I sought.

I had been in the room with a trance medium who was trying to teach a friend of mine, Carl Wiggins, how to go into trance. I slipped into a relaxed meditative state such as I had experienced as a child. Right after that I began to "see." (The kind of seeing I mean happens when your mind forms images and impressions.) At first I was startled, but it was familiar At last I was reclaiming what I had put away as a child.

THREE
Psychic Counseling

As my friends became aware of my hard-won breakthrough into "seeing" and "knowing," they began coming to me for help. Then their friends started coming. Soon I had so many clients that I switched to doing psychic counseling fulltime. For the past thirteen years it has been my only profession. Psychic work is incredibly exciting to me, especially when I can discover one more new way to use this sensitivity that we all possess. It is frontier work, and with each new element that comes to light I want to see how far I can go with it.

Naturally in the beginning I practiced on light things, where there was no great weight of responsibility. However, at lunch one day a friend asked me a question that brought me up short. Herself a lawyer's wife, she asked me in the presence of another attorney's wife, "Will 'Jean's' husband pass his bar exam so he can relieve the burden of my husband's practice?" Well, my first heavy feeling was no, and I thought, hey, I don't want to say that in front of this man's wife. So I suggested it was a pretty important question, and that I'd like to meet the man before answering. Later, as I talked to him, I became sure that he was going to pass his bar exam. Then why did I still get the strong no? At once it became clear that he wasn't going to help carry the other man's load because he was in the military reserves and he would be going off to Vietnam with his group.

That taught me that you have to be intelligent with this. If you're still caught up in this idea of the lightning bolt, thinking just whatever comes to you must be given directly to the client, then you may often be pulled in the wrong direction. Forget the mumbo jumbo about "powers" and "gifts." Good psychic counseling requires that you bring to bear all your resources of intuition, intelligence and experience. Certainly my earlier success in business has helped me to be a better counselor. I don't understand how people can attempt to counsel others without having first learned to cope with the world themselves.

There are two keys to psychic counseling: interpreting and translating. First of all, you must be able to interpret for yourself the pictures, symbols and impressions that you are sensing. Then, equally important, you must be sure to translate this information so that you are certain it means the same to the client as it does to you. If you say to a woman "I see you with an older man," you must check out her idea of an older man. An eighteen-year-old may be picturing someone twenty-two. If you tell a man 5'7" that you see him concluding a business deal with a tall person, he may picture someone six feet tall. A six-foot client, however, may think of himself as average in height and spend weeks on the lookout for a giant tycoon!

There may be no more meaningless phrase than "a large sum of money." If someone tells you they see you getting a large sum of money, for heaven's sake ask for more specific information. If your most pressing need is for fifty dollars to pay off a long-distance telephone binge, your mind will focus on fifty dollars. If your heart's desire is to own your own home, then you may think of $20,000. Always be sure to question until you know precisely what is meant. Unless psychic material is presented in such a way that it helps you in your life, I believe it is just a waste of time.

I had not been in this field very long before I realized that there were three big questions with which I was wrestling. It was absolutely necessary for me to work these out before I could have confidence in my ability to help people. The big three are:

1) Am I just reading minds?
2) How much can I responsibly tell people?
3) Am I interfering with free will?

"What if I'm just reading her mind?" I'd wonder to myself. "If that's all I'm doing, what good is it?" Every time I found myself worrying over this crucial question, I would get an answer to it. I would tell a client something, and he or she would say that it was totally wrong, absolutely impossible. "Your husband's mother was an opera singer," I would say. Perhaps a little chuckle would accompany the woman's denial. After all, I had been right about other things. Later would come the telephone call: "How could you have known that? We've been married twenty-four years and he never told me that his mother had a brief career before settling down to become a housewife!" In those early days, no one questioned me more than I did, but every time I needed a little proof, I'd throw in something of this nature and I would get an answer.

Even more difficult to deal with was the question of how much to tell people. What if I see something that is sure to be dreadfully upsetting to my client? In the beginning I tried a number of approaches. For a while I told people only what seemed to be nonthreatening. Later I tried to limit my remarks to what I sensed they were willing to hear. Every so often I would give someone the total picture because it seemed important to do so.

I worried about having told a psychologist the exact time her husband was going to die. He was ill, but was not expected to die. After telling her, I fretted, thinking maybe I should merely have said that his health didn't look too good. But after he died, I got a call from her and letters from other members of the family thanking me for pinpointing the time of death. One son would have gone overseas if he had not known; instead, he visited his father for the last time. Another son, who was not on good terms with his father, came from out-of-state to make peace. When I looked at all the lives affected positively by that knowledge, it convinced me I had done the right thing.

Experience has provided me with an excellent guide on how much to tell. It is very simple. I never tell anyone anything unless they come to me and ask. If they ask, I know they will be able to handle whatever they get. I have learned that I never tell a client something that, down deep, he or she doesn't know already.

The third question with which I struggled in the early days had to do with free will. Am I interfering with a person's free will by giving advice and making predictions? It soon became obvious that I had nothing to worry about on that score. People only listen to what they want to hear. If they don't like what they're hearing, they simply shut you out. Later you may hear some interesting stories from them.

An attractive woman, obviously on the lookout for a husband, brought me a photograph of the man she had been dating for several months. I took one look at his picture and told her he was a liar, a cheat who was already running around with other women, and generally no good. She agreed with me! "Yes, I suspected as much. Sometimes he stands me up and then calls the next day with a trumped-up excuse. I looked at her directly. "But I think you are going to marry him anyway." She flushed, but answered with a stubborn air. "If he asks me, I'll marry him. Things will be different then." I could see that she did not really believe that. I went a step further. "I see also that you will divorce him if you do." But her face was set and it was clear she was going to do what she wanted to do.

Later, she did marry and then divorce him as I had predicted. She went through all that, though she knew his faults even before she came to see me. But it was her free will to marry, suffer and divorce. I try to help my clients to avoid making the same mistakes over and over again, but I no longer worry about interfering with their free will. If they aren't ready, they won't accept my advice anyway.

I do counseling in all areas of life, and the majority of people who come to me have been referred by someone who has already used my services. In recent years, because of the publicity attending my police cases, many people read a newspaper article and then obtain my telephone number from directory assistance. Others are referred by doctors with whom I have worked in the past. No psychic needs to advertise.

People often come to me when they don't really have a specific problem—maybe just a gnawing feeling of dissatisfaction, a notion that things could be better for them or that something is missing from their existence. One man came to me with those kinds of feelings and, through counseling, shortly realized that he had been in the wrong profession for years. His parents had guided his choice when he was a young man, and he was stuck with the results. Of course, his chronic discontent had affected his wife and children. Once the source of his dissatisfaction was apparent, the solution was obvious. He began taking night school courses more suited to his desires and talents. The enthusiasm generated by this change carried over into the rest of his life, and his wife and children responded quite differently to the more positive person he had become.

In personal counseling, I begin by taking you back to the time of your birth and seeing what programs were being played around you. (I use the word *program* to describe what we are and what we are sending out, or broadcasting, to the world. This will be dealt with more fully in a later chapter.) I look at your mother and father: What were their programs toward themselves, toward each other, and toward you? This information comes to me through images and impressions that appear in my head. I share them with you so you are able to understand your parents' needs and problems and how they affected you. Then I move forward to check out how the parental programs have influenced your life to the present. Have you been fulfilled in your work and your personal life? Possibly you have also been strongly responsive to the programs of other people in your life. If I see that the programs you are receiving are leading you to negative results, I try to make you aware of this and how to stop it.

In marriage counseling, I do much the same thing, seeing each partner individually at first. Then I put them together and try to explain to each of them who the other person really is. I help them see what they have done to each other. Then they go away and try to work with what I have given them. Sometimes they just can't resolve things, particularly if they have what I call an "elephant and tiger" marriage. This occurs when an "elephant" has married a "tiger" and each keeps trying to view the other as one of his own kind, without realizing that his mate is of a different "species" altogether.

Recently a couple came to me in a last-ditch effort to save their twenty-five-year marriage. They had had difficulties ever since the beginning and had tried in vain to work things out. Psychically, I picked up what was wrong at once. He was an attorney, highly cerebral, who suppressed all his emotional responses. She was a nurse who dealt with people's emotions all day long. It came down to my saying to the husband, "Mel, you're a tiger, and you insist that your wife be a tiger, too. Well, she's a camel, or maybe an elephant, but certainly not a tiger!" Knowing this did not repair the damage done by their long-term conflict, but it helped them to see that neither was really at fault. As a result, the divorce was an amicable one.

So often, when I am doing marriage counseling, I will psychically pck up the difference in their ways of broadcasting. A partner who operates on a mental level may say "Don't be ridiculous!" He doesn't mean that his wife or her thoughts are ridiculous. But I have to explain to him that "When you say 'Don't be ridiculous,' your wife feels you are belittling her—that she is always slightly ridiculous to you." Often the husband is astonished, because he had used that phrase without emotion and is bewildered that she reacts so violently to it. Then the wife will usually speak up and say "You make me *feel* ridiculous when you say that, and I am always hurt by it." People can go on for years, completely misunderstanding the words and actions of the person they have married.

When I do premarital counseling, I try to find the area where there is most likely to be conflict and warn the partners ahead of time. A man asked me whether he would be happy with the woman he planned to marry. I did a psychological profile on her, checked out their programs together, and concluded the marriage had a very good chance of succeeding. I warned him about only one thing. "She can have her own business, or stay home and be a housewife, but she must not become involved in your business." A year and a half later the man returned, very upset. "I did the one thing you told me not to do. I let her help out in the business, and now I've lost everything—the business, my money and my wife." For reasons not apparent on the surface, free will led him to do the one thing that would spell disaster.

Marriage counseling can have its lighter moments. One day a woman came in and, when she had sat down, I described her first husband. Then I said "Oh, but you married again." I described her second husband. "Oh, but you married again," I said once more. This went on and on, to my growing astonishment. The lady finally admitted she had been married seven times! I asked her if she realized that she had repeated the same mistake with each marriage. In all those marriages she had not learned to look at the something within her that was triggering the problems. It was something that went back to her parents' marriage. The last I heard, she was marrying for the eighth time. I hope that one works.

Business counseling is a big part of my work. Often I am asked to evaluate an investment. Psychically I look into who owns the company and how it is doing. You might think an investment counselor would do as much, but an investment counselor can only base advice on the *past* performance of the company, while I can look into its future as well. A company might currently be solvent, but I can pick up the factors within it that might send it into bankruptcy. And I can see how the business is doing, even though they have not issued a financial statement. After looking at the facts I have picked up psychically, I might say "This woman rubs you the wrong way, but she is basically honest, so get in touch with that. She is a real worker and will make you some money." Or I might say "Here is a man who is outwardly a success, but he does not have the tenacity to stick to anything, so he'll stop short of completion and you'll lose the money." I help my clients to see why the investment will or will not bring them dividends.

Several companies won't hire their top people without my seeing them first to determine if they are right for the job. I chart them just as I do for personal counseling. Then I see if they will be able to handle the job in question. Sometimes the person is better for another sort of job within the company.

I have worked with one electronics firm since its inception. Initially, the partners came to me with a list of names and asked me to choose the one that would be most successful with the public. When they were looking for a location, they came to me with addresses and I picked the location psychically. Each time they launched an electronic component, they came to me with a list of customers. I picked the companies which would buy the fastest, the ones that might conceivably become competitors, and those that would not be interested. This saved them marketing time and money. They are in a gorgeous new building that I foresaw five years ago when the company started. Nowadays I counsel them on the feasibility of companies they wish to buy. The relationship has been profitable for them from the beginning.

Sometimes business partners come to me because they are having problems with each other. I find that I have to do essentially the same with them as I do in counseling a married couple. Two men who owned a real estate company had never felt comfortable with each other. They didn't use the same approach to anything. I showed each one that the other got good results using his own methods. I showed them the motives behind their actions, which healed the breach that was beginning to develop. Partners need to see each other's positions so the company does not suffer.

Sometimes people come to me before they go into business together and I can see that the partnership won't work out. I'll point out the differences and often they will admit that they sensed something like that but didn't want to face it.

One man who sees me regularly has three full office staffs, plus at least a dozen businesses in addition to his major one. I have literally counseled everyone from his housekeeper to his top executive. He is a person who is very aware that just one negative vibration in his office can affect the entire business.

Another field that interests me is child counseling. When the child is young, I can work with the parents just from a photograph of the child. After puberty, however, the child must come to me voluntarily or I won't work with them. When the child has passed the age of consent, I take each parent individually, then the child, and explain them all to each other. I think it is very important not only that the parents understand the child and his or her needs, but also that the child realize his mother and father are people with their own problems in life. Too often parents get stuck in roles and conceal from their children that they, too, have needs, fears and desires.

Recently a woman came to me with a picture of her daughter, whom she felt was lacking in intelligence. She was contemplating sending her to a school for slow learners. The mother then showed me a picture of her other daughter, who, she reported, was extremely intelligent. "Wait a minute," I said. "I just checked out both of the girls and they are equally intelligent. But the little one is like a powerhouse without fuel. She is running so sluggishly that she cannot perform at top capacity. I see allergy problems . . ." "Yes, Kay, she does have allergies." As the mother talked on about her daughters, I noticed that she was unconsciously broadcasting a program that the younger was not as smart as the older. I pointed this out to the mother and was able to make her see that her program was actually affecting her daughter's performance adversely. When the woman left she was already viewing her younger child in a new light. She had also changed her mind about sending the little girl to a special school where, as sensitive as she was, the child would only have come to be slower and more apathetic.

At the opposite extreme, I have counseled the parents of a son so hyperactive that people could hardly bear him. I told his parents that he was a "physical reactor." By this I mean that he reacted to incoming programs physically: If he felt anger from someone, he would hit them or go into a frenzy. On top of that, he loved to take everything apart to see what made it work. I recommended that he participate in lots of sports, and that a part of the.garage be set aside where he could hammer and saw to his heart's content. At my suggestion they took him to a pediatrician who found that the boy was a hypoglycemic who reacted by being hyperactive. I encouraged the parents to try to accept their son as he was, or they would have an increasingly unhappy child.

During our session the parents mentioned that they were redecorating the boy's room, which would now have a red rug and draperies. I told them that red was the absolutely worst color for an already physical child. Right then and there, the mother called the store and re-ordered the items in blue, which is a soothing, mental color.

A year later, the parents returned to tell me that the difference in their son was incredible. He had made friends and was excelling in school. He was still a physical reactor, but without the extremes that had made life so miserable for all of them.

Occasionally I do counseling for unborn children. Maybe I'll see that the child will be born with a certain allergic reaction, and tell the parents to have the pediatrician check that out after birth. Perhaps the child will be born with potential dental problems, so it should be taken to the dentist early. Many times I have outlined the personality of the as yet unborn child.

I am very accurate in predicting the sex of a child. One obstetrician made notes on his patients' charts as to what sex I had predicted. After checking me out for several months he jokingly said he was thinking of hiring me himself. The only time I find it difficult to predict the baby's sex is when parents or grandparents have a preconceived notion as to which sex they want. Then I have to wait until I am alone and tune in on the child without "interference."

Often I have been able to tell a woman who fears she cannot conceive that she will bear her own baby. When she telephones to tell me about the arrival of that longed-for child, it gives me great pleasure.

In addition to my seminars and lectures, I have answered people's questions on TV and radio call-in shows. Once, at the end of an East Coast TV show, I said "There's a lady out there who has tried desperately to get in touch with me, but I don't feel that I've spoken to her. I'll go over all the calls after I'm through, because I feel she is terribly upset." I described her appearance and promised to call her.

Later I went through the calls, selected the one, and phoned immediately. "Are you the lady I just described on TV?" I inquired. She assured me that she was. "Look, I know you are very upset, but your sister is not going to die. I see your brother-in-law saying 'Thank God, thank God' and taking her home from the hospital." The woman said they had just phoned to tell her to come at once if she wanted to see her sister alive. I responded that she would certainly make herself and everyone else feel better by going, but I knew that her sister would recover. "Well, I hope you're right, Dear," the woman replied dubiously. "At least you've made me feel a little better."

About a month later the woman phoned to say that a short time after she arrived at the hospital her sister took a turn for the better and she had stayed to see her brother say "Thank God" and take her sister home. To this day I have never laid eyes on the woman; it all happened through television.

People have asked me if I prefer one kind of counseling. I feel equally comfortable with men, women and children, and I like to have variety in my life. It is not necessary, either, for me to feel a special rapport with a client in order to be able to counsel effectively. You learn to go past the person's program in order to arrive at the truth.

I do like to help young people find themselves. Recently I counseled a young college student who had been caught in the act of armed robbery. With his permission I provided the lawyers with material they could use in court on his behalf. The judge decided not to send him to jail, but to have him counseling other young people as I had recommended. The young man went on to graduate with honors. I felt good about that.

FOUR
The Psychic Detective

PSYCHIC HELPS FIND BODY . . .
PSYCHIC'S UNCANNY VISIONS KEY TO FINDING
MURDER VICTIM!

In the headlines, I am always finding a body. No wonder an interviewer recently asked me, tentatively, "Do you, uh, ever find anybody *alive*?" I do find living people, of course. It's just that right now my "body count" seems more dramatic to the news media.

Though the publicity is recent, my first police case occurred nine years ago. A woman came to me about the disappearance of her mother. As we talked, I knew that her mother was dead, and that her body lay somewhere near the foundation of the house. I also saw that she had been murdered by her husband, my client's stepfather. I told the woman, but she couldn't get the police to act on the information because there was no evidence of foul play. I moved to another state shortly thereafter and heard no more about the case for a while.

31

Then the house where her mother and stepfather had lived was sold. The new owners decided that the cement slab laid for the garbage cans was too near the house and in an inconvenient place. So they dug it up. And the murdered woman was there, buried under that slab.

Since then, I have worked on many, many cases of disappearance, murder and kidnap without any fuss being made. It was simply another facet of my varied work as a psychic counselor, until the Sheriff of Calaveras County, California told the news media that I had been instrumental in solving a case. The next morning I went downstairs for breakfast and found two rival television crews waiting for me.

Russell Drummond was an elderly man who had suffered several strokes which had caused a slowing down of his thinking processes. His family took him with them on a camping trip into the rolling Sierra foothills of Calaveras County. On September 2, 1978, he wandered away from the family campsite, and a search by one hundred people failed to discover any trace of him. His family continued to look for him until winter set in, making the search impossible.

Finally, in the early months of 1979, a relative of the missing man telephoned me to ask if I would try to "psych" his whereabouts. Upon hearing the circumstances of his disappearance, I began to place the man mentally, a process I think of as "mind-reaching." It consists of experimentally placing the mental image of the person in a variety of surroundings.

I became aware of an area where the ground was covered with a vine-like kind of underbrush, and I saw that Mr. Drummund had sat down, had a stroke, and slumped over as he died. I was able to give precise directions to the place where he lay; it was in an area that had already been searched. I also mentioned that there would be a new, younger sheriff who would find this man, and that he would be accompanied by three other people when they found the body. The family then told me that a new sheriff had just taken office. They took a tape recording of my instructions to the authorities.

The officers told me later that when they first got the tape, they thought they would just run through it and see if anything matched up. After hearing it, and realizing that the material was accurate, they decided to go out to the area and look around, with the idea that they would return the next day for a full-scale search. Instead, following the instructions on the tape, they walked directly to the body. The new sheriff had three people with him at the time.

Many months later, when I did a law-enforcement seminar in Santa Barbara, three representatives from the Calaveras County Sheriff's Department were there. They were among the most perceptive of all those who attended, being about 80% accurate in the tests that we did. Solving a case with a psychic is immeasurably aided by the receptiveness of the officers who are working on it. When they are willing to use *their* awareness to interpret what I am saying, we can proceed very smoothly. In the few cases where officers have sat defiantly with arms folded, daring me to tell them something of value, they fail to hear what I am saying and derive no real benefit from it. The Calaveras County people are outstanding in their ability to tune in to one another and to work successfully with intuitive material.

Because I respect my client's right to privacy, I would never release information to the press. In this instance, the case was a matter of public record, and the Sheriff was so enthusiastic about my work that he released the story.

The resultant publicity led the parents of a missing child to telephone me for help. Victoria de Santiago, eight years old, went to the grocery store with her three-year-old sister on the afternoon of February 3, 1979 in Fresno, California. When they came out of the store they looked for their dog. A car pulled up, and the two men in it told the little girls that they had seen their dog. Both little girls were observed getting into the car.

Five hours later, the three-year-old was found wandering quite a distance from where they had been abducted. There was no trace of Victoria.

When Victoria's parents told their local police department that they were planning to see me, the department sent along a young, very intelligent detective named Tim McFadden. The parents, McFadden, the pilot of their chartered plane, and a number of relatives came together to my office. As soon as I was shown a picture of the little girl, I knew she was dead. I told the mother that I was sorry to have to tell her that Victoria was dead; the more I realized the condition of the child, I had to ask the mother to leave the room.

Working with Detective McFadden, I began to trace the route of the abductor. Here is where the knowledge of the officer is essential in interpreting the impressions that I get. I said that I wanted to go north out of Fresno on a highway that had three numbers rather than two. McFadden told me there are two such routes. The one I wanted made a very sharp turn to the left, which I thought meant a turn to the west. He asked what I saw there, and I replied that I could see mountains. He said that the only one with mountains ahead did indeed make a very sharp turn to the left, but it actually changed course from a northeasterly direcion to more directly north.

Then I felt that we were no longer on a well-traveled road, because there were not many cars going by. I was seeing a cultivated field. "This person is surprised that you have not already found the body, so don't look for her in a grave or in a house," I said. The road here sits higher than the surrounding fields, sloping down to culverts on either side. I could see her body lying on its side on the righthand side of the road near a solitary tree. She wore only white socks, and had been brutally raped and beaten. Looking past her, I could see a windmill some distance away. I kept feeling that a poultry farm was in the picture. The letter "S" also figured in it.

Tim McFadden flew back to Fresno with the material that evening. He was aware of the facts I had mentioned that were known only to the police. Ten hours later, the police found Victoria's body. She was lying just as I had described. The mailbox on the property where she lay had the letter "S" on it. The poultry farm and the windmill were nearby. McFadden was so pleased with the quality of my help that he had the tape transcribed, underlining the parts that I could not have known through ordinary means, and presented it to the Justice Department. When the officers and family spoke to the press, a deluge of publicity ensued.

One result of this is to bring positive attention to the work of professional psychics, and to lend this field the credibility it deserves. That is gratifying to me and serves the broader goal of stimulating people to trust their own intuitive resources.

Another result, naturally enough, has been an increase in the number of detective cases on which I am asked to consult. Unfortunately, most of these cases involve brutality and violence. I could be overwhelmed with sadness and misery if it were not for three things.

First, I am protected by my philosophical understanding of the continuity of life. Human beings have chosen to live in terms of past, present and future, but the universe encompasses all of these simultaneously. What we see as death is actually just another rite of passage in our total entity's existence. The chain of life is continuous, and this knowledge helps me to put traumatic incidents in perspective.

Second, in my psychic detective work I consciously emphasize my practical and analytical sides. So far as possible, I lay aside my emotions and concentrate on solving a problem. I usually request that I work directly with the law enforcement teams rather than with the family. It can be confusing and distracting to pick up the heavy emotions of people in crisis, and I must insulate myself to some extent in order to serve them.

Third, it is characteristic of me to try to make sense out of things. I may be a natural-born detective, in that I love digging for the facts, finding the continuity or the context in which all the elements make sense. I get quite excited when I think, hey, here's something we can use. Getting so involved in the search for answers is my greatest protection against the often-tragic nature of the facts.

From the Secret Service and the FBI to the policeman on the beat, there is currently great interest in the use of psychics for crime detection. These officers have a willingness to listen, and will go to great lengths to check out psychic material when they see a professional attitude on the part of the psychic. Occasionally I run into some initial resistance.

Agents working on one FBI case had become so soured on psychics that when they heard the family had hired me their response was "Who is the kook this time?" But after I had spent an hour with them they were won over by my business-like approach and became my active allies. Apparently they had been tormented by a series of oddballs, one of whom insisted they spraypaint a cross on the wall before work could begin!

So-called psychics who phone police to volunteer "information" after reading about the latest crime in their newspapers are doing both the police and the victims a great disservice. Usually lacking the pertinent facts on which the police are working, they insert their personalities and their thoughts into the case. It is precisely like having ten people run up to the scene of the crime and walk across the evidence. When I am called in on a case where this has happened, I have to take each one of these volunteers and go through their thoughts, decisions and predictions to see whether they were on the right track. I pick up their feelings on the case along with everything else, so I must then painstakingly eliminate all of this before I can go to work. The same thing is necessary if the family has hired a series of psychics before me. It is both more sensible and efficient to pick just one person and give them the time to do the job.

When I am working with detectives for the first time, I always explain how my work relates to what they are doing. I am only there to add to the total knowledge about the case. There will be no lightning bolts, no sudden illuminations. I am going to work on their case with everything I've got. I tell them I am only as good in their field as the hours I spend.

Everyone wants me to work miracles. There have been a couple of cases in California involving one man committing a series of crimes. The police departments brought me in for a day's consultation, but then did not follow up on it. Ideally I should be brought in at the beginning of a case and be available each day to the investigating officers. Then if I sensed that the criminal would strike again perhaps I could try to see where, so that the police could stake out the location.

In one particular case I was able to tell the day on which a rapist would strike again, but I had to work on other cases and was not brought back. The date arrived, the rapist struck again and was not caught. I felt very sad and frustrated, but there is only one of me and I cannot come into a case uninvited.

One of my dreams is to train a corps of dedicated individuals to do psychic crime detection. Right now I am trying to help people in the various law enforcement agencies to develop their own psychic potential to the fullest. I give seminars and classes especially for the police. My main objective in these sessions is to encourage the police officers to be aware of their own ESP.

In one seminar, I told the law enforcement group that I would look out the window and select a vehicle, and then they were to tell me the color, make, and other pertinent data. We went through several of these, and then on the next one a man from the D.A.'s office got very excited and yelled, "I can feel it! It's flat . . ." and he trailed off in confusion, not able to think of a car without curves. His hand was still "feeling" the flatness in midair. He *did* feel it. It was a pickup truck and he was sensing the truck bed.

When officers are on their way to the scene of a crime, I want them to get in touch with the fact that they already sense what they are going to find. A seasoned cop routinely uses a combination of intuition and intelligence. That intelligence has been rigorously trained, and now we can begin to train the intuition in the same way. I teach these men and women to recognize ESP when it happens, instead of just flying blindly. Not only will they be more effective police officers, but also it will help to assure their safety as they approach dangerous situations.

One San Jose police officer, Tom Macris, has come a long way in developing his psychic capabilities. He is the only fulltime police artist in Northern California, and in the past two and a half years he has worked on four hundred and fifty felony cases.

It was while Tom was a motorcycle cop that his sister told him about a course she had taken in which people were trained to develop and use their paranormal faculties. Skeptical initially, Tom went to a lecture demonstration and was impressed when one of the instructors "read" Tom's absent girl friend, including the fact that she suffered from a chronic degenerative disease. He took the course. After a while, he discovered that he could do readings himself. Though he experienced this, Tom found it hard to accept because he couldn't integrate it into his daily life.

Actually, he *had* occasionally used his intuitive knowledge with some success in cases where he had little or no help from witnesses. A teenage rape victim had her arms chopped off by her assailant. She walked miles, bleeding profusely and in a daze, to get help. Tom had to conduct an interview in her hospital room the day after her first operation. The girl was still in shock. The circumstances were, to say the least, poor.

Still, Tom felt himself drawing the face of a man in a very free-flowing manner. He simply "went with the flow." From that drawing, which was published in newspapers and shown on TV, a witness came forward who recognized the suspect as a former neighbor. She called the police and gave them his name and last-known address. Very shortly the man was in custody and he is now serving a prison sentence.

The drawing that pleases Tom most is one he did of a rape suspect from a "description" by the victim—a deaf mute! It went so fast that he was suspicious of its validity even though the woman kept giving him nods of encouragement. The suspect was subsequently identified when another police officer saw Tom's picture and recognized the man, a street character whom he knew by name.

When he read about me in the newspapers, Tom had an intuitive flash that we would soon be working together. Sure enough, we met on the case of a triple killing at a shopping center. That I was a developed psychic using my abilities in a straightforward way caused Tom to reassess himself. He tells me that hearing my views helped him to get over the last obstacle to using his own abilities. We agree that you don't have to be a "born" psychic. It requires neither a bump on the head nor twenty years in a monastery.

We do have something unusual in common. The police artist and the psychic are both used as last resorts. A police artist is used only when there is no evidence other than a witness' or victim's glimpse of the suspect. Up to this point, I have been brought into a case only when all else fails. There is a certain camaraderie in that.

I seemed to be, for Tom, the catalyst that allowed his natural psychic abilities to be manifest. The first thing he noticed after he met me occurred as he was trying to draw the face of a rapist from the descriptions of one of the five victims. He "saw" some of the man's features *before* they were described. Since then he.has become more and more able to see pictures of suspects in his own mind. He is now paying more attention to his mental images. Together we have experimented with creating pictures based entirely on psychic impressions.

Both Tom and I envision the day when that corps of specialists in psychic crime detection becomes a reality. He is eager to bring his experience as a police officer to the task. If we could train just two or three officers in each city, it would be very interesting to see the effect on crime in this country. Going an important step further, I hope that one day we might use the psychic detective to prevent crimes.

Because crime detection is such a new field for the psychic, there are few precedents or guidelines. I am learning by trial and error. For example, I have learned never to pass along information to the police through the family. Giving it to them directly, I can be sure that nothing is lost in translation.

I have never studied criminology, so there is much to learn. The more I know about weapons, motives, and many other things, the quicker I can catalog all the facts of a case and move to the heart of the problem. Actually, I would like to work with just one law enforcement group. Then together we could formulate procedures that make optimum use of both kinds of experience.

When all the dust has settled and the case is closed, the victims still have to go on living. "Larry," a client whose wife was murdered, was with me recently. He had been working with the police since the crime occurred, sifting through leads, trying to think who could possibly have wanted her dead. I said to him "At the moment, Larry, you're so busy focusing on the crime and finding the murderer that you're not experiencing all the grief you have inside." "I know it, Kay," he replied. "I'm dreading the end of the investigation. When I go back to my old routine and have to return to that empty house every night, I'm afraid I'll be overwhelmed by grief and loneliness. May I come to you for help as I try to live without her?" I assured him that he would be welcome.

And so, after the last pieces are fitted into the puzzle, the psychic detective becomes a counselor once more.

FIVE
A Balancing Act

Think of yourself as a radio. You are both transmitting and receiving all the time. A clear understanding of the way this operates is the first step to developing your own psychic abilities. Why be satisfied with functioning as a crystal set when you have the capacity for quadrasonic and beyond!

The physical parts of your psychic radio are the endocrine glands. Each of these glands has an emotional, mental and physical function. It is very important that each of your glands be working properly and that your endocrine system be in balance if you want to use your psychic sense optimally.

The human body has seven centers (or chakras, as they are known in Eastern thought), points of psychic energy at which the physical body and the astral (or subtle) body connect. Each of these centers relates to a particular gland or organ. In addition, we have come to realize that each center and its gland is represented by one of the colors of the rainbow, as well as by a particular musical tone. This may seem a little strange at first, but when you think how intricately our entire universe is interrelated, it is only to be expected.

43

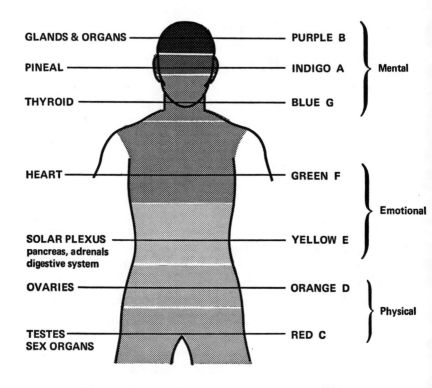

GLANDS & ORGANS ———	PURPLE B ⎫
PINEAL ———	INDIGO A ⎬ Mental
THYROID ———	BLUE G ⎭
HEART ———	GREEN F ⎫
	⎬ Emotional
SOLAR PLEXUS ——— pancreas, adrenals digestive system	YELLOW E ⎭
OVARIES ———	ORANGE D ⎫ Physical
TESTES ——— SEX ORGANS	RED C ⎭

BODY CENTERS, COLORS, AND TONES

The color chart which depicts all these related elements is in the form of a rainbow, with red at the bottom ranging to purple at the crown of the head. This chart appears in full color on the back jacket flap. One way to balance yourself is to focus on each color in turn. We will start with red.

RED

This vibrant, exciting color rules the sex glands, or gonads. The sex drive is survival in its purest form, so this first center is related to survival. It rules anything that is exclusively physical. It is the seat of our instinctive "fight or flight" responses. Uncontrolled rage is red.

A healthy sex gland gives off a pure red vibration. If our sex glands are unhealthy, their color vibrations become muddied and weak. Nutritionally, vitamin E is necessary for the glands that red rules—especially for athletes and other people whose work requires great physical stamina.* The musical note associated with the color red is C. If you are exposed to red color while listening to a C tone, your sex glands will be stimulated to vibrate in their purest resonance.

A handsome young artist came to me for counseling. Everything proceeded smoothly until his comment at the end. He said he was surprised that I hadn't mentioned the fact that he was oversexed. I looked quickly to make sure my exit wasn't blocked. Then I told him that I had seen no indication of his being oversexed, but would review his physical aspect to make sure nothing had escaped me. No new information appeared.

I explained to him that as an artist he fell into the category of physical reactors. This means that he reacted physically to his world by painting. He had been meditating deeply for a year and a half, which stimulated an increased re-

*The information in this book is not intended as medical or nutritional advice. It is data gathered through my experiences and study. Anyone who wishes to follow up on it should consult a medical doctor.

sponsiveness on all levels including his hardworking physical/sexual ones.

I suggested that we slow down his red intake and add blue (mental). This would not only balance his physicality, but also make him a more creative artist. When I explained that red was stimulating both physically and sexually, he suddenly understood his problem. It seems that his entire bedroom was red, including the hall leading up to it. "Well, with all that stimulation, it's a wonder you didn't die in bed!" I blurted, to his surprise.

A can of blue paint applied to the bedroom gave the needed balance. He could have coupled this with meditating under a blue light for a while. Once he realized what had happened, he made the necessary changes and was soon back to fulfilling his creative ability on canvas.

My daughter is a physical reactor, being an artist. Even before she started showing signs of her talent, I intuitively dressed her in red. (At the time I thought it was because I was a redhead and believed that I could never wear red.) One of my sons, on the other hand, is a mental reactor. While he did the obligatory things, he was the least athletically inclined of my three boys. Ignorant of the importance of color at the time, I put this baby in a red bedroom. He banged his head against the bed day after day, would not sleep, and almost completely wore me out.

He was a natural engineer from the day he was born. Often the entire household was awakened in the middle of the night by the sounds of the blender, washing machine and other electrical appliances all going at once. He would have been a happy child in a blue room, because he was always a person who would sit down, think and create. He was sending me the message by banging his head in response to that red wall when he was only nine months old.

ORANGE

In many ways orange is like red (being a combination of red and yellow), but it represents the physical and sexual, with emotion added. It rules the hormones in both sexes and the ovaries in the female. This second center perceives others' emotions and gives and receives sexual feelings. Its corresponding musical tone is D. I will almost always find an imbalance in this area if a woman is on birth control pills; it can also be changed by the menstrual cycle, pregnancy and hysterectomy. Anything that causes a man to worry about his manhood, or a woman to question her femininity, will throw orange out of balance.

People with strong orange responsiveness are also physical reactors, but they add intuition. Actors, sculptors, writers—all those who wish to express physically what they feel—can be in this group. What is nutritional for the reds and yellows will also nourish orange.

A woman whose husband was notoriously unfaithful to her came to me suffering with cancer of the liver. As we explored the programs of her parents, it came out that she was a dutiful child to a very strong father. She told me that she would never do anything to upset him, but always respected and obeyed him. His image was carried on in her husband, whose characteristic way of dealing with her was to do as he pleased, no matter how it affected her or the children.

This woman felt she had failed as a wife and as a mother. She had failed as a parent, she said, because she was so like her father. She wished she could be more like her husband, because nothing bothered him. These two statements told me that she was aware on some deep level that her father was a bad parent, and that she believed her husband cared too little about his family to be bothered. With all of these strong feelings unexpressed, it is no wonder her orange center got so clogged that she developed cancer.

Cancer, to me, signals a body out of balance, so I suggested she see a doctor who had been doing excellent work in regressing cancer through the use of meditation. The next time, I wanted to know how it turned out. "Oh, I believe in everything he's doing," she said. "But I couldn't do that." "Why not?" I asked with dismay. "Because he uses four-letter words," was her reply. I knew that this man used earthy language to shock his patients into listening and caring. Now she was setting him up as another male figure who could control her life, or death. (His choice of language was so "vile" as to prevent her being cured with his help.)

Her husband did not like to acknowledge the cancer and would not talk about it. So, dutifully, she waited until he was out of town and then died in her bed alone.

YELLOW

This is the main tube in your psychic radio. The third center, located in your solar plexus, is your power center and the locus of psychic energy. Everyone talks about "gut feelings." When you get bad news you feel it first in the solar plexus. Where do you get butterflies? Same place. It is the door to your being, and it must be under your control. You must be able to filter out what you don't wish to receive, and to handle what you *do* want.

Physically, yellow rules the digestive/assimilative system, the pancreas and the adrenals. The related musical tone is E. Necessary nutrients include vitamins A and C, potassium, some enzymes and hydrochloric acid. We often find that a highly sensitive person who doesn't know how to control his sensitivity has depleted some or all of these. Prolonged stress or extensive use of the adrenals may cause an inability to assimilate protein, calcium, iron and the B vitamins, among other things.

One woman had been a counselor for many years and

was a beautiful, humanitarian person. She came to see me because she was in bad shape physically, especially in the digestive/assimilative and adrenal area. A knowledgeable M.D. was willing to sit in on my counseling, and together we discovered a lot that could be done to heal this woman's abdominal region. I told her that she should completely shut down her yellow center (through imagery).

"My dear, I cannot tolerate yellow," she said. "Whenever I see a piece of yellow fruit, or even a yellow tissue, I become quite nauseous." Through thirty years as a counselor, she had never learned to release the programs of other people from her solar plexus. It was as if she had been shoveling sand into a room. Every time the yellow light went on, the door opened and she would shovel in another load of sand. Even when the room was already full she continued shoveling until finally the walls burst.

On one level she knew that every time she was exposed to yellow her solar plexus opened for more to be crammed in. Since she did not release it mentally, emotionally, or psychically, her physical counterpart reacted by vomiting and developing adrenal problems. I told her to stay away from everything that stimulated that area, including the color yellow, until health and harmony were restored. When that was accomplished, I assured her, yellow would no longer make her turn green.

Anyone who works with the yellow center will find they react strongly to overexposure to the color. I have a yellow blotter on the desk where I sit to counsel, and sometimes I need to replace it temporarily with a blue one. I become oversensitized, things come at me faster than I can comfortably assimilate them, and I have to give myself a break. Similarly, I have lived in many houses and, even before I started this work, always painted over a yellow kitchen. To be sensitive that early in the morning was hard on me, and it was no more than a desire to protect my solar plexus that prompted me to repaint.

Kitchens aren't the only place where yellow can wreak havoc, as another woman showed me. She came to me because she couldn't sleep, though until recently she had dozed off as soon as she hit the bed. Psychically I saw that she had changed bedrooms, so I asked her about it. Sure enough, she had recently exchanged with her daughter, moving from a blue room to a yellow one. She was so sensitive she couldn't sleep in it. It opened her solar plexus to everything going on around her. Repainting was, once more, in order. In fact, in many cases I could give out a standard prescription: "Take one can of paint and call me in the morning."

Yellow is only good, I think, in rooms where one spends a limited amount of time. People who are already highly sensitive should stay away from it. When in doubt, avoid it.

GREEN

Green is related to the heart, and the fourth center encompasses self-love, love for others, and compassion. It responds to the musical note F. An imbalance in this area can be due to physical problems with the heart or to emotional heartbreak. I have seen cases where green has been out of balance in a person for a long while because of a "broken heart," and the person eventually developed problems with the physical heart as well.

Green is the color of humanitarians. These people have great empathy with their surroundings. In fact, the pain of others is picked up so acutely that it is almost self-preservation that brings them to choose a life of service. This can be overdone.

A woman came to consult me just after her married daughter had inherited some money. The mother thought her son-in-law was spending too much of the money, and her daughter was not demanding that they invest the money in certain ways, and on and on. This woman was a strong green reactor, so much so that she had never noticed that she frequently offered help when nobody wanted her help. Finally I said to her, "You know, I'm not really interested in what's going on with your daughter unless she wants to come see me, but I *am* interested in what you are doing to yourself because of this great need." I suggested that she volunteer to work with some agency serving those who really need help and are asking for it.

An imbalance in green leads not only to rejection by people who want to express their own autonomy, but it also leads to a weakened person who compulsively serves others to the detriment of his or her own life. Balanced greens produce teachers, doctors and counselors—anyone with a compassionate aspect to their work.

BLUE

With the final three colors—blue, indigo and purple—we move into the mental aspect of our being. Blue is associated with the fifth center, the area of the throat, and relates to the thyroid gland. Its musical tone is G. Basic blue is strongly related to the practical mental functions, such as solving problems and giving or following instructions. People who are very strong basic blues can seem nitpicky, but they are much appreciated as accountants and technicians, among other jobs requiring great precision.

Blue has been medically proven to slow down the heartbeat and other bodily systems that race under stress. As blue is a natural tranquilizer, I feel that calcium is related to it because of similar tranquilizing properties. Magnesium and B complex vitamins nourish the blue area; protein provides nutrition and also has tranquilizing qualities for those who operate on the blue level.

We have succeeded in helping some hyperkinetic children by having them sit quietly in a room with a blue light, two or three times day, drinking a glass of milk mixed with protein powder. This helps them nutritionally, and the blue slows down the senses so that the yellow is not so strong. Natural sensitivity is not destroyed; rather, it is monitored and regulated. These children are still physical reactors, but they can develop some forethought, so that they no longer punch their mothers in the nose or kick their shins. We slow down their machinery, and we don't use drugs because they tend to make the body sluggish while the sensitive reactions remain the same. Drugs seem to make those reactions still harder to cope with. Each child needs individual medical evaluation, of course, so don't fail to consult a doctor if you are trying to cope with this problem.

A woman who was having difficulties getting along with her husband showed me his picture. I told her that this was a man who would absolutely have a fit unless people did things "right," and by the book. He was in the restaurant business, and had hired a number of people who were emotional responders—that is, they were "people" people, who were more interested in relating to the customers than in being precise about their work. This would seem to be appropriate for the restaurant business, but the poor man was distraught because he could not get his employees to follow the rules he had set up. I told the woman he would either have to hire others like himself, or go into a line of work which required practical, precise qualities. Perhaps he should sell his restaurant and purchase a hardware store, where everything could be neatly categorized into bins. A career change can be a saving grace for a person like this, and for his marriage as well.

INDIGO

Creative thinking is the keynote of indigo, which is related to the sixth center, or forehead. You may be familiar with the idea of focusing on the "third eye," the area just above and between the eyes, during meditation. This is an area of visualization where creative thinking is at its most intense. Indigo is related to the pineal gland, and its musical tone is A.

An engineer is a good example of a blue person. If he is also working in indigo, he will go beyond the simple construction of components and produce highly creative designs. He will tap the lake of universal consciousness and incorporate new concepts into innovative products or structures.

A young woman was working in television production, staging various programs. She was unhappy with her job and the people with whom she worked. I told her that her ability was in the creative part of the business, that her frustration derived from working on others' ideas instead of bringing her own into fruition. She was holding back in the blue area instead of moving into indigo, where her greatest satisfaction lay.

PURPLE

People who resonate to purple are usually extremely inspirational individuals, responding to their universe in highly spiritual ways. This group also includes the geniuses who bring from universal consciousness revolutionary theories and inventions previously unconceived by humankind.

Purple is associated with the seventh center, the top or crown of the head, the area of pure inspiration. It contains the pituitary gland, which is often referred to as the master gland. This gland responds to the musical tone B.

If they are balanced in all seven colors, purple people can take their beautifully inspired knowledge and create works that add a deeper meaning to the printed page or to the canvas. Purple is the color of the highest yogis and religious leaders who are in touch with the vast knowledge of universal consciousness.

People who operate in the purple area are frequently so

far ahead of their time that they seem remote, sometimes even stupid. (Albert Einstein was not a good student.) They are out of balance if they are unable to bring their intuitions into the world in which we live, for we are meant to function within this structure to fully express our humanness. I always encourage this type of person to bring it out—it's not worth anything unless you share it.

A man and his wife came for counseling, and I said to him "You're capable, but you're not using it. You should be living in the purple. You'll never be happy or contented in this life if you don't exercise some of that." His wife looked at him in complete surprise. Almost embarrassed, he said "Yes, I have an idea for a machine that will save many man hours in the type of work I do." His wife was completely unaware of this facet of the man to whom she'd been married for years.

RAINBOW

Everyone has all seven colors, and yet one or two of them will seem to express particularly well how the person relates to the world. The ideal is to achieve a balance, consciously or unconsciously, in which the other colors are well represented. People who succeed in achieving this balance within themselves seem to us well-adjusted or "centered."

A psychiatrist may be a blue and green blend. He or she wants to help people on a mental level. The great artist is often a combination of red, orange and the blues. Not satisfied just to splash color on canvas, the artist brings back creative ideas through the blues and purple which will open doors to the universe in viewers' minds. The doctor who blends green with indigo and purple becomes greater by combining the need to help people with knowledge gained in medical school and truly creative, inspirational thinking. If yellow is added, there will be unusual diagnostic skills as well. You can begin to see that each color enhances the others in making us fully human.

People who come to me are seldom in balance, though occasionally I will see someone who tries to offset working all day in the mental and emotional areas by engaging in active sports. With new clients, I begin by charting their colors. First I sense which color characterized them at birth, then what color predominates at the moment of our interview. I then look at their work to see if it corresponds. I consider their spouse to see if they are the same or different, and if they harmonize. Last, I check whether the client is over-stressed in one level and about to "blow a fuse." This provides me with a context into which I can fit our ensuing conversations and gives me an extra dimension in which I can be of service.

It is important to allow, in fact encourage, people to experience their reactions. If they are reds, physical reactors, they must express themselves in that way before being moved into blue. This is why I suggest workshops in the garage for hyperkinetic children; they must be able to work off their physical impulses even as they are being brought into better balance with their blues.

I see this need to experience all levels in terms of an irrigating system, where there is a water pump at the bottom and the water flows up through our centers as if through pipes. If the pump keeps the water rising, we are mentally alert, physically active and emotionally alive. If little faucets at the red level drain off all the water in physical activity, then the emotions and the thoughts will never get enough. Or, if the red level is dammed up, the rest of the person will suffer. This is true of the other levels as well. And if one goes, make no mistake about it, the others will follow. A balanced flow of energy throughout is absolutely necessary to health and vitality.

Sometimes people tell me they have been to an aura reader. "She said she saw a lovely shade of pink around me," they will say delightedly. "What does that mean?" Well, I really don't know. If the aura reader didn't tell the person what that meant to her, how could I know? What does it give the person as a tool in self-understanding?

Others tell me that they have learned to surround themselves with white light for protection. But when I ask them how it works, they don't know. People accept information of this sort without questioning. I explain that since white light contains and reflects all colors equally, it is simply a device for balancing oneself. Also, if you see only white light, you create a barrier to experiencing the individual colors and are less open to others' programs. I used to have a predominance of black in my wardrobe. Now I know that I was compensating for my extreme sensitivity by dressing in a way that blotted out the colors I might otherwise receive. (Black absorbs all colors, so that none of the rays are reflected and our eyes don't see them.) When I came to understand and control and balance my own colors, I stopped having to choose black dresses.

Ignorance is our downfall. The only way we protect ourselves is through knowledge. Question everything. Learn. Grow. Be a rainbow.

SIX
Broadcasting

With balanced energy flowing though all levels, and colors harmonizing beautifully, the psychic radio located in the solar plexus is in perfect condition to do its job of broadcasting. This involves both the receiving of others' programs and the transmitting of our own. We make these psychic connections without words, though words may be involved, and we make them with everyone with whom we come in contact, though the ones that affect us most will probably be those between us and our families, friends and co-workers.

All of us have an important invisible dial which is set from birth at low, medium or high. This setting represents the degree to which we characteristically pay attention to the broadcasting that is going on right under our belts.

Everything in the universe emits a "program." We often call this a vibration. It consists of what has happened to that person, plant, animal or object: what it is made of, what it has been exposed to, what it has ingested and what it has known. This is your moment-to-moment experience and it is all there—nothing gets left out. It is what you transmit to the rest of the world.

Low

Low receivers are not aware of any of this. Their universe is very limited and they don't hear incoming programs. These people could be called insensitives. You can say over and over to low receivers "Please don't do that, it bothers me." Even though you may put a great deal of emotion or force behind the words, they will never hear you. They may think you mean it just for the moment, or the day, and will keep on doing it for the next fifty years, or until the divorce, whichever comes first. You may keep complaining, but they never hear beyond your words, if that far. They simply don't receive.

There may be reasons for this. Low receivers could be insensitive because any or all of their seven glands are not working properly, so they are not attuned to what you are saying, and even your words are not retained for any length of time. Or they could have been high receivers at birth, but because the programs received were so loud or so negative, they turned their receivers down. If they are not receiving because of a physical malfunction—a blown tube—then a "repairman" should be called in. Maybe their hearing is off, or their reflexes are unbalanced, both of which can be associated with the glands.

The naturally high receivers may have tuned out because of something traumatic in their lives—parents who fought constantly or were too domineering, for instance. A child might have blocked not only his or her own suffering, but that of others. A bitter divorced parent or grieving widow can broadcast at unbearable volume. The child turns off in self-defense and, years later, still has not turned on. The result is a low receiver. It is important not only to recognize this type, but also to understand why, if possible.

Medium

Now we come to the average person. This is the kind of person who will go through most of his or her life and never be aware of a psychic happening unless struck between the eyes by it. For example, something happens to a man's mother and she sends out a strong program: "I am in pain" or "I need help." This may cross the screen of the medium receiver for a fleeting moment and then get lost in the shuffle again. He returns to his normally scheduled program until someone calls and says, "Mother had a heart attack." Then he'll say, "That's strange; she came to my mind quite vividly this morning." But it usually doesn't register in his mind that the "coincidence" might mean something. Some people will get the urge to do something: "I just have to call my mother." They'll talk about for the rest of their lives, telling everyone "I knew the moment she took sick. Isn't that amazing?" If you are reading this book, you know it isn't.

There is a lot more where that intuition came from, but average receivers have learned to regulate their volume and they aren't getting it. If someone came and asked for help, they would turn on and tune in to their requests, deliberately increasing their volume to get everything. This is in direct contrast to low receivers, who wouldn't be aware that someone wanted something from them, even if they were hit over the head with it. When medium receivers have finished tuning in, they turn their buttons right down to medium again and get back to everyday work.

These people are usually well-balanced. If something does happen to throw them off it can create problems, because they are used to being in balance. It's like driving at 55 mph all your life, then finding yourself at speeds beyond 150. Later we will talk about how this unfortunate state of affairs is sometimes induced.

HIGH

The happy medium receiver is in a good place compared to the high receiver. People with their dials on high hear their own and everyone else's programs. If they are hearing thirty or forty programs at the same volume all the time, how are they going to decide which one is their own? Talk about an identity crisis!

If a boy gets up happy in the morning and his parents are not, it won't take long before he is just as unhappy as they are. Being new to this emotional game, he doesn't realize it is because of them. He only knows that at one moment he is happy and the next moment he is not. Because his personal program is on the same level as everyone else's, how does he choose? A child is not old enough to know that they are not all his own programs. This we have to teach.

We have to be open with our children, so they know where the program is originating. We have to let them know when we are happy and when we are miserable, and that takes honesty. Nothing is more confusing to a child than to feel tension or unhappiness in the room, only to be told untruthfully that "Mommy and Daddy are feeling just fine," especially when Mommy and Daddy have been slugging it out mentally or physically. The child will then decide that, if *they* are fine, it must be *him*. A confusion can begin in this way that will follow him into adulthood.

We have to realize that children like this are extremely sensitive to their world, and we must help them understand this for themselves. Otherwise they are emotionally going to drive around at 150 mph all their lives, and one day they will not make a curve.

I feel that the vast majority of hyperkinetic children are on the high-receiving end of the scale. They receive so fast and so strongly that they don't have time to think about it, and they act it out right away. Their experience is a constant hit-the-solar-plexus-act-on-it and they don't use judgment with it. I'd like to see more research done on the solar plexus area and what high reception does to the body of a child. I feel that many hyperkinetics and epileptics, as well as child geniuses and prodigies, are high receivers. There seem to be larger numbers of sensitive children these days, but perhaps we are only more aware of them. There could be environmental reasons, too." Some doctors theorize that pollution, by causing mineral and mental imbalances in the body, can oversensitize us. Diet and other sources may do the same thing.

Please remember that sensitive children grow into sensitive adults.

REACTORS

Not only do you have a volume control, you also have another invisible gauge that reads "physical," "mental" or "emotional" reactor. You are born with this gauge, too, and it indicates how you react to the programs you are receiving through your psychic radio, no matter what the volume. These categories are vital, because failure to recognize and accept the level (color) and reaction someone is born with can often lead to the square-peg-in-a-round-hole syndrome.

I wish there was a school system that incorporated this knowledge in dealing with children. By recognizing children for what they are, the schools could help them to channel their flow towards self-fulfillment. Each child's potential is directed by this inborn response to his world.

THE PHYSICAL CHILD

When a physical child feels happy, he or she wants to display it in a physical way. They will come up and hug you to satisfy this need. They will enjoy having physical release, like

REACTIONS

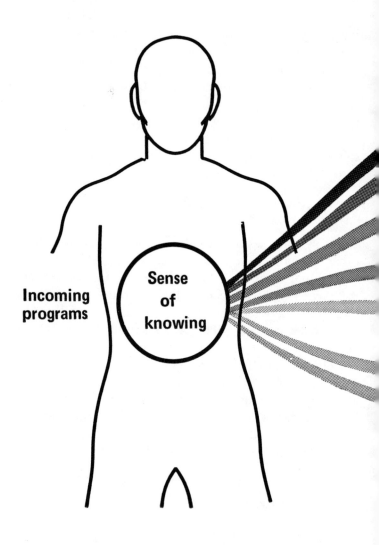

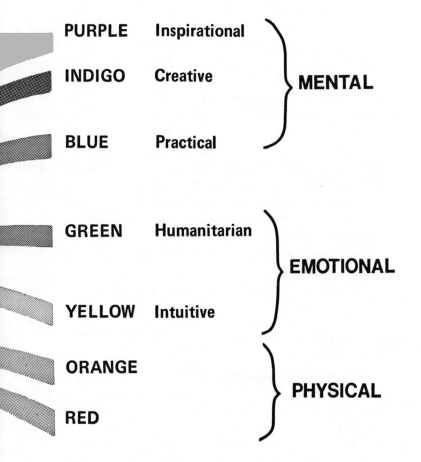

PURPLE	Inspirational	
INDIGO	Creative	} **MENTAL**
BLUE	Practical	
GREEN	Humanitarian	
		} **EMOTIONAL**
YELLOW	Intuitive	
ORANGE		} **PHYSICAL**
RED		

dancing, singing, sports, painting and writing. Their bodies are used to express the programs coming through them. When the program is unhappiness, the physical child will lash out—as angry babies do when they thrash their arms and legs. They will slap, kick or bite their mothers.

I am well aware of this individual, as I was one as a child. While I sat in my high chair at age two, my father asked me where my other shoe was. I said I didn't know, and said it quite emphatically. When he repeated the question, I was so indignant that I slapped him across the face with my tiny hand. Dad was equally a physical reactor, as he revealed by his hand on my bottom a minute later.

Extreme examples of physical reactors are the married people who beat each other, or tear up the house, or abuse the children. A compulsive example might be the woman who scrubs every floor in the house to "get it out," or the classic scene of an angry driver speeding his car to its mechanical limits on a mountain road. Even a jogging session or a long, quiet walk are methods used by a physical reactor to express himself.

THE EMOTIONAL CHILD

When this child feels a program of hate, he or she will fully return that hate through the emotions. In order to restore their balance, emotional children will strive to transform that source of hate. They will also have terrific empathy, duplicating the emotions of others. This response makes them natural humanitarians, because they are not able to bear suffering; it is replayed too clearly through their own systems. Making the world a happier, better place will naturally make them happier, too. They respond to books, movies, pictures and animals. This child makes the best doctor or nurse, veterinarian or social worker. He or she is a good environmentalist, too, because they also respond to the needs of the environment. The sight of pollution or drought scarring the countryside makes them feel personally wounded.

THE MENTAL CHILD

These children react to their world logically and analytically. For them, our existence is based on facts. There are three different levels of the mental child.

Basic Blue

These children bring programs up from the solar plexus to the head and analyze them until they are in acceptable form. Then they can cope with them. They take the practical approach to a problem, using knowledge as a tool for comprehension of the world. They follow directions easily if they seem logical. If Mother says two plus two equals four, they accept it without further debate. They make excellent accountants, scientists, engineers and organizers.

Creative Indigo

A child born in this category may accept that two plus two has equalled four up to this point in history, but he or she might decide to take it a step further and see what else two plus two could become. They take practical applications and add creativity to them. Their universes are unrestricted and unlimited, with the result that they often build a better mousetrap.

Here in creative indigo the mental and physical reactors begin to mix. This means they will paint better pictures, write better poems, than the purely physical child.

The other side of this coin is the daydreamer. These children seem to be dawdling and accomplishing nothing. This is not true, as they are accomplishing a great deal, but it is within themselves. These daydreamers find very little to relate to in the factual world, so they withdraw into themselves.

Inspirational Purple

This child takes creativity into uncharted areas. A child of the creative mental level usually starts with some point of reference and works from there, but the inspirational mental child doesn't have a point of reference. He goes immediately into unthought-of areas. Ideas conceived on the inspirational plane usually have no precedent. Da Vinci was out there with his concept of the airplane, tapping the inspirational. Thomas Edison was another member of this club. He said that the only time he doubted was when a group of engineers told him what he was doing was impossible. He found their opinions surprising, because up until then he had been doing it with success. He wouldn't have known it was beyond the reach of man if they had not told him so.

AT HOME

Suppose we were to take three children representing the physical, emotional and mental reactors and put them in a family situation. It is seven in the morning and breakfast is on the table. The children are just finishing and ready to start for school. Their parents had a fight last night and their mother is still feeling very negative about it. She is unjustly harsh and irritable toward the children, in an attempt to ease her own frustration and anger. They are unaware of the squabble, but are getting the fallout anyway in the form of their mother's feelings. Here is how they react according to type. (Each type could either be a girl or a boy.)

Physical Reactor Child

He wants to retaliate by hurting his mother to the same degree she has hurt him. Instinctively, he bites her or slaps her. The lesson that this is socially unacceptable behavior is learned through a good backhand from his mother. Since that doesn't work, he may kick the cat, or fight with his brothers and sisters. He may take it to the playground or schoolroom where, more than likely, the teacher will introduce him to some more social refinements through some form of punishment.

Now, with all this pent-up hostility, he is marched into class and told to be quiet, sit down, and think. In his frame of mind, wriggling around seeking release, this is hardly the condition under which clear thought is produced.

Emotional Reactor Child

She feels her mother's anger and duplicates it. She may have gotten up very warm and loving and happy with the world, but now there is this anger in her solar plexus and she has to react to it emotionally. The usual result is that the two feelings mix and she bursts into tears. Her whole day has become unbalanced and it is more than she can cope with. No matter how she tried, she couldn't seem to bring one feeling to the foreground and be of a single mood, so she cries.

The one course of action open to her is to try to appease her mother. If the mother feels better, the girl hopes she will, too. If that doesn't work, she will go to school with a stomach full of confused emotions, only to be expected to sit down, think, and do as she is told. That is hardly possible with such inner chaos.

Mental Reactor Child

This child is the lucky one. He looks at his mother and makes a checklist of the situation:
1. Mother is angry.
2. She is probably angry with Dad.
3. She is angry with me.
4. Since I am not the cause, I'm not going to worry.

And off he trots to school. The situation is going to throw him only if he can't figure it out, or it is constantly repeated, wearing down his mental defenses. Even so, if his first class is math, he will find release for his inability by working out facts and figures.

AT SCHOOL

If society, and therefore the school system, were really aware of the importance behind these distinctions and how they affect children and their schoolwork, schedules could be set up like this:

Physical Child

His first class would be painting or gymnastics. He could draw pictures of his mother, or at least release his physical aggression in sports.

Emotional Child

Her first class would be a discussion group. She could talk about her mother and how she feels toward her. Or she could be put into a happy room with quiet activity. Anything to give her emotions another chance to balance before cold facts are thrown at her.

Mental Child

We have already suggested a math class for the mental child, but a psychology class would serve as well. He could sit and analyze the whole problem, solving it to his satisfaction.

Because we are living in a situation where convenience prevails over individual considerations, children grow up forcibly molded by parents, teachers, social beliefs and stresses. Often they alter their natural selection of a career or lifestyle, sometimes for economic reasons, and get locked into a job not suited to their natural vibration. They make good money, but that will not still the grawing feeling of unfulfillment. It manifests frequently in physical problems at the level that they are fighting against. The results show up in businessmen with ulcers, movie stars who have "everything" yet have nervous breakdowns at the peak of their careers (or commit suicide), and housewives who are afraid to go out of the house.

Suppressions such as these at any age level need to be cleared out daily. Chapter 11 describes the method I have developed as a release mechanism to balance and free your being of any repressions or inexpressions.

Remember, most people are a combination of more than one color. The same applies to reactors. Generally, people are a combination of physical-mental, mental-emotional and so on, rather than just one category. However, one aspect will always dominate, with the other two for balance. When I counsel, I always check to see what sort of reactor the client was at birth and whether he or she has remained true to it. If not, trouble may be brewing.

PAUSE FOR STATION IDENTIFICATION

I sense one or two raised eyebrows out there. You are muttering "This is all very fascinating, but when do I start learning to be a psychic?"

In using a radio, you won't get any action if you don't know what the various buttons and dials are for. You familiarize yourself with all the controls before you use it. If you expect to repair it yourself, you will need to know all about the mechanism. Otherwise, you are working in the dark. I believe that if I tell you how some of this works, you will turn out to be a better psychic. One who has no mysteries about his apparatus—how to turn it on, control the reception, and turn it off—is obviously in a much better position to succeed than someone who has no idea how it works. All this will make you the master, not the victim, of your intuition.

SEVEN
Interference

When changes in reception occur, they can throw you far off balance. Someone whose switch has been on medium may be completely bewildered by a switch to high, and remain out of balance for some time. Someone who is on high, and managing as well as can be expected, may suddenly go to pieces mentally or physically if the load increases too sharply. There are many factors, both emotional and physical, which may contribute to this undesirable possibility.

YELLOW

Once again this color crops up. A person who spends too many hours in a yellow room will accelerate sensitivity. This might be fine for a low receiver, disturbing for a medium, and disastrous for a high. Medical science has proven, through experimentation, what metaphysics has known for centuries; namely, that blue slows down receptivity and yellow opens it up.

71

THE MOON

Ah, if only the moon *were* blue! It would make things a lot easier for everyone. Doctors have discovered that both the full and the new moon create quicker responses in people: more bleeding, more pain, and more irrational actions. Emergency-room personnel and police officers can tell you stories about the increase in traumatic incidents during the full moon. More babies are born when the moon is full. Both these facts are well-documented.

People are also much more receptive during this time. The full moon really affects me. I'm not usually conscious of the lunar changes because I don't bother to check my calendar, but on a night when I lie in bed with my eyes wide open and all the programs in the world pouring through me, I can be sure that behind my drapes the big, round satellite is shining down.

ALCOHOL

Liquor can open the solar plexus. Some people have a few drinks to loosen them up, relieve some of the day's accumulated stress, and relieve their inhibitions. They drink to relax and get more in touch with other people and what is going on around them. That's fine if you are a low receiver. If you are a high receiver, alcohol can get you in a lot of trouble. Have you ever awakened in the morning with a shocking memory of what you did the night before? You wonder why you did it, knowing it was so alien to your being. If you realize that you were opened by alcohol and vulnerable to everyone else's programs, you might be able to understand it. You might even discover that it was your Aunt Grace's secret passion to dance on the table. (She is so glad, the next morning, that *you* did it and saved her the mortification.)

DRUGS

All the stimulants, whether coffee, alcohol, or other drugs—
from the potent ones like LSD to the little "harmless" ones
like diet pills—can turn your volume up to the fever pitch of a
rock concert. The youth of today say they "turn on," and
they really do. They increase the level of their reception and
play out the roles around them.

If you take LSD with a group of people who are all in perfect balance and looking only for positive programs, it may
be fine, no problems. How can you get into trouble doing
that? When you go out the door hours later your radio is still
at its highest, and it is not going to turn down until all the
drugs are out of your body. This may take weeks. (Simple
aspirin can take four days to get out of your system.) During
this time, your radio no longer has a volume control for you
to turn down. You get among other people and find that one
has financial problems, another's marriage is on the rocks,
and still another is in poor health. The same drug that gave
you all those great feelings because of the positive programs
around you as you were taking it, now turns on you.

You don't know what is happening. You felt so good and
now life is utter hell. It can literally make you jump out of a
window. I know that if we investigated some of the drug-
related suicides which remain unexplained, we would find
the victims were playing out someone else's program. In fact,
I've had the experience of just such a case. It was a man who
committed suicide for his father.

This man's father had been a chronic emotional patient
for years. He lived four states away from his son. Normally
the son received his own program loudly and clearly, enough
to override anyone else's program. He knew, on a conscious
level, that his father was ill, but it didn't interfere with the
son's life or work. He was a classic medium receiver.

One day his father had a particularly bad bout and went
into a critical depression. The mother called her son. She

asked if he would spend part of his vacation out there with them, helping to cheer up the old man. The son said yes, and from then on part of his energy was going out to his father in anticipation and worry.

The father, at the other end, knew his son was coming and returned the vibration. He was also broadcasting feelings of his illness. Ordinarily, the son could cope with these feelings because he knew of his father's condition and understood it. But a random factor entered the picture. In an effort to lose weight, the son took diet pills prescribed by a well-meaning physician. Suddenly he had no volume control, and he received not only his own program but also a lot of others, including one that said he didn't want to live. This increased as he stayed on the pills. He felt that life wasn't worth living. There were no problems in his marriage or his business—nothing but this unaccountable desire to die.

One Sunday, he and his wife went to brunch at a friend's house. He wasn't a heavy drinker and he only had a couple, but added to the pills it boosted his reception unbearably high, opening him wider than ever. The death vibration became so strong that he went home, took a pistol from his nightstand, and shot himself.

Four states away, his father had hit an all-time low and was being committed to a hospital for suicidal depression. Because of the fuzzy grip the son had on reality, due to the pills and liquor, he never fit those pieces together and realized he was feeling his father's depression. He simply picked up the program so strongly that he just had to act it out.

I always argue with my drug-culture acquaintances that I can get just as high through meditation as they can with their drugs, and I have the bonus of being able to control what I receive. But one night, during a dinner party, someone offered me a marijuana cigarette and I agreed to smoke it, just to prove to myself that there were no surprises coming. Wrong.

I discovered that it accelerated my flow of consciousness

to such a level that I had to wrestle constantly to retain perspective and contact. I am used to receiving the flow at a rate that allows me to put it into useable form. With the marijuana I had to dodge things as they came at me, or I would have been squashed like a psychic bug on the road by every plea for help.

Suddenly I became so depressed that I went off to my bedroom to try to get in touch with myself. My day had been a nice one and I had good friends around me, but I was still being compelled to self-destruction so strongly that I could hardly resist it.

I was trying to cope with this feeling and cook dinner for my waiting guests when the telephone rang. It was a producer from Hollywood whom I had counseled, and he was in a totally suicidal depression. As soon as he spoke, I knew where my program was coming from. He said he was at the bottom and didn't know who to turn to. I told him that I certainly knew what he was talking about. I then asked him to please hold it in check until the effects of the drug had subsided and I was better able to help him. What I suspected about marijuana had proven true.

DIET

I've seen some people so dazed from extreme diets that they weren't all there. Their theory is that in order to be sensitive, you must become a vegetarian. In an ashram in the Himalayas, this kind of diet might be fine. I am in favor of any kind of diet that makes you feel your best, as long as it is balanced.

Once I was at a party in Washington, D.C., with an outstanding medical doctor who understood the effects of nutrition on sensitivity. We stood talking to a woman who was so unclear that my head simply spun, just listening to her. Soon my friend said quietly "You're a vegetarian, aren't you?" She

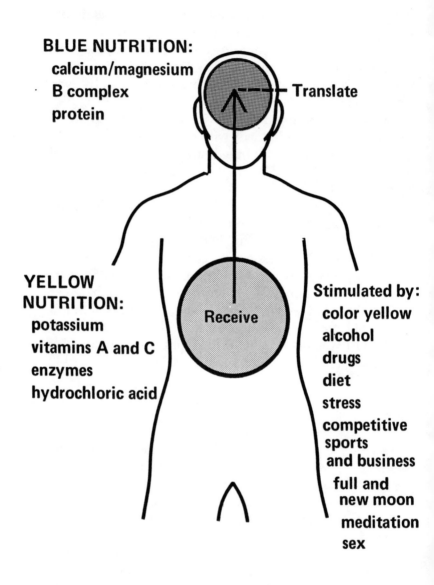

BLUE NUTRITION:
calcium/magnesium
B complex
protein

Translate

YELLOW NUTRITION:
potassium
vitamins A and C
enzymes
hydrochloric acid

Receive

Stimulated by:
color yellow
alcohol
drugs
diet
stress
competitive
sports
and business
full and
new moon
meditation
sex

said yes, she had been on a diet for about seven months, solely under her own supervision. After he had asked her a few more questions, I asked him how he could possibly have known about her vegetarianism. Was it his psychic faculty? No. He told me that her lack of rational conversation was a direct result of an umbalanced vegetarian diet. He said that he could tell one every time.

So I began to watch for the symptoms he described and, sure enough, a great many people who became involved with Eastern disciplines or occult philosophies started a vegetarian regime. This is not implied as criticism or discouragement of either vegetarians or the Eastern beliefs. But true vegetarians have learned to balance their diets with the all-important factor: protein.

Many novices simply drop everything from their diet except vegetables and soon are flying as high as kites, only without any string. With no control, they are buffeted by anything coming through the Universe. They may get some good views up there, but without the string they can't come back down to the conscious level and work with them constructively. Protein is the brain food which helps us to translate our knowledge like that. Balance must be stressed in a vegetarian diet through soy beans, nuts and dairy products. These foods conform to the vegetarian principles they are trying to embrace, and still provide some "string" for their psychic kites.

STRESS

Have you ever been in an automobile accident where your own quick action was the only thing that helped you avoid catastrophe? Instantaneously you received information: "Turn here, press this, move there, turn this off." I'm sure you are not in the habit of having accidents and few of us have trained for the Indy 500, so where did that instant response come from? It was stress that fired off the rockets of your adrenals, releasing a lot of adrenaline into your body, which stimulated all your mental and physical resources to get you out of danger. (Remember, the adrenal glands are in the solar plexus, where they receive all kinds of intuitive information.) Under some conditions, like the auto accident, that response from your adrenal glands is protective, healthy, even life-saving. But a constant bombardment from stressful situations exhausts the adrenals through over-stimulation, throwing the whole psychic mechanism out of balance and producing bad physical results as well. Our only protection lies in understanding the process, avoiding stress insofar as possible, and handling what is inevitable with as much intelligence as possible.

In my counseling of people who are critically ill, I have yet to find one whose adrenals are not depleted. Whether the depletion is a product of the illness, or the illness is a result of the depletion, I don't always know. I do know that the two seem to be related. So I believe it is unwise for anyone to deliberately increase adrenal stimulation without knowing what they are about.

Since the solar plexus is the porthole to our adrenal glands, psychic people are common sufferers of over-stimulation. This must be prevented by learning how to control your center. You can use the technique of shutting it off to avoid unnecessary stimulation and being certain to get the proper nutrition for replenishing what is drained away by overuse. Hyperkinetic children experience this problem too, and only after being helped to slow down can they learn to deal with the incoming information and react at a useable pace.

EXERCISE

Exercise, especially competitive sports, stirs up the glands. The stimulation will be only as vigorous as your exercising and will slow down again afterwards. We often find that while we are exercising, precognitive and intuitive thoughts pop into our minds. This happens in competitive sports particularly, and it is not always a bonus.

The young man who works in the blue, the mental type, can look at the game objectively while in his physical activity. He uses his mind to plan strategy, apply strength, and defend weakness. His mind tells him how best to use his body. Should he lose the game, his mind works with facts and circumstances in such a way that it allows him to accept the defeat.

The red man, the physical reactor, goes into the game with all his physical machinery at concert pitch and plays to the fullest, purely reveling in the activity. After the game, win or lose, he can drop with satisfaction because he has had a good workout. Maybe he has put a hole through the locker room wall to shed the overtones of defeat.

But the intuitive man, yellow, whose adrenals are not only stimulated by physical exercise but also by sensitivity, has a slightly different program. He feels the excitement of playing, but he also picks up the thoughts of defeat which the other team is projecting his way. He may be as magnificently physical as the red, as intelligent as the blue, but he works with his intuition. The result is that when the line of opposition players runs toward him, he is encompassed by a wave of "Kill, crush, defeat!" Yellow promptly responds to this stress by over-stimulation of the adrenals. If he is not aware of the source of the program, he may not shed it in the locker room, but feel hard hit long after the defeat. Furthermore, he feels his depression plus that of all his teammates.

One young athlete was a prime example of this. He was not really a physical reactor, but had forced himself to many athletic achievements for his parents' approval and in memory of his deceased brother, who had been an effortless athlete. This young man had worked under the wrong vibration for years, amassing adrenal over-stimulation not only through exercise and stress, but also through his natural intuitions. Everything was screaming "Wrong!" at him, but he was suppressing it. The tragic result was cancer.

There is one special type of exercise that encourages psychic awareness and I'm certain that you will be glad to know about it. Sex. Many people find themselves experiencing intuitions and even visions during sexual stimulation. This is because sex stimulates all the glands and such overall tuning up results in a heightened state of awareness. I'm rather amused at all the new seminars with titles like "Increase Your ESP for Sexual Sensitivity." When we accelerate the functions of all the glands, the natural result is better sex. We are also going to get an increase of emotions, mental stimuli, creativity, bodily functions, everything. But that isn't as exciting a sales pitch as sex these days. Even the Eastern yogis who abstain from sex do exercises that stimulate the sex glands, because they know all the glands must be working in order to have total use of the *kundalini* (as they call the centers). We call it sensitive awareness; it is the same thing.

MEDITATION

It always upsets people when I associate meditation with interference. They think meditation is so wonderful and special—how could it throw them off balance? Like anything else which opens your psychic centers and awareness, it can unbalance you if not properly handled.

People come into my office after taking meditation and awareness courses and tell me "It was so good at first. I was really getting in touch with myself. But now I am having such highs and lows, I can't handle them." They want to know why this marvelous approach that had been beneficial has turned on them.

If you are hearing your own program more clearly through meditation, you will also hear the programs of others more clearly. Meditation turns up your volume, but it does not select the station. This is overlooked too often by course instructors. People must learn to identify whether the programs coming through are their own or someone else's. If this is not done, they can get into trouble. I am very much against indiscriminately taught meditation and mind-control classes which do not warn people about the increase in their sensitivity and give them the tools to control it.

EIGHT
Programs

Now that you have an understanding of your own psychic mechanism, how will you be able to use it? We have talked about the physical parts of your psychic radio—the glands, with their centers and characteristic colors. Related to this is the knowledge that you may be either a physical, emotional or mental reactor. We have discussed what can happen to your radio if the volume control is too low or too high, as well as the causes of these conditions. And throughout all of this we have emphasized the need for balance and harmony.

With your radio in tune, let's turn to selecting the programs you want to broadcast, and exploring how to clarify what you pick up. The three principal steps involved in your program schedule are *receiving, translating* and *releasing*. These are all part of being psychic—of doing psychic work—and they are all vitally interdependent on one another.

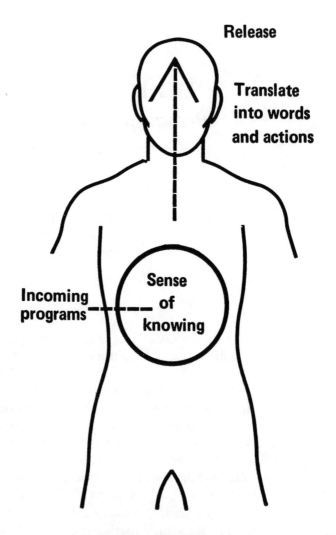

Release

Translate
into words
and actions

Incoming
programs

Sense
of
knowing

BASIC PSYCHIC
PROCEDURE

PSYCHIC RECEIVING

You know you are a receiver, and that what you are receiving is often someone else's program. But that is not enough. You have to *understand* the program that is playing loud and clear through your solar plexus. Suppose you are really down, have the blues. You need to do the following:

1. Look at yourself. Any reason to be sad? How's your life, your love, your love life? All right? Lost your job recently? Any hormonal changes? Other physical problems? The chances are it's not *your* sadness if the answers are all no. So...

2. Look around you. Check your family, by thinking about each one. Loved ones. Friends. A friend you've spoken to or thought about lately. Do any of them have a problem? Is someone grieving? If so, you've hit it, maybe even thought it out. You have the who and the why; now you can cope with it or forget it. You will find the feeling attains perspective or fades away. If, however, this doesn't work out...

3. Look ahead. There is always the possibility that you are experiencing precognition and the sadness will come to you, or others, sometime in the future. If you feel something strongly, consider making a note of it. Accuracy can only be measured by results. We so often let these feelings pass us by. If we paid attention, we might find that we are experiencing consistent psychic awareness.

I cannot emphasize enough the importance of recognizing which and whose programs you are receiving. Many of them may cause just a ripple in your day. Others may be prolonged until something happens to finish them off—either a sudden understanding of their source or a response acted out (such as the man who committed suicide for his father). There are many degrees of reaction in between.

While my daughter Cindy was living in England, our blond Afghan dog Tamara started having trouble with her hindquarters. I took her to the vet to be checked out. He called me later and suggested I see the X-rays. Both lungs were full of tumors, surgery was impossible and the only solution was to put her to sleep. Tamara was an active, affectionate pet that we had had for years and we are a family of animal lovers. After much consideration, I agreed to the doctor's suggestion, but I could not bring myself to write Cindy about it. So I waited a few days, trying to regain my inner balance. I should have known better, because Cindy and I are in such close communication that we practically play each other's programs by the moment. Trying to keep it from her, even in England, was futile. And not without consequence.

Cindy had a cocker spaniel named Alex she had bought in England. He came from Northern Ireland, and with all the violence and negativity that country is experiencing, it was small wonder that he was snippy. (After all, animals respond keenly to vibrations on an instinctive level.) He was loving too, in many ways. But he was unpredictable, overridden by his profound suspicion of human beings. When I visited, he would fight me for right of passage to the bathroom at night because it was beyond his sleeping place. Yet the next minute he might crawl up on my bed and beg to be loved.

While visiting an English vet one day, Cindy mentioned Alex's unpredictable personality. He looked at his pedigree and told her that all males out of that particular bloodline were "minus a marble." He had owned one himself and found him so untrustworthy that he had finally been forced to put him down. Cindy replied that Alex was not that bad and she could handle him herself. So she did not consider putting him to sleep, but the thought had been planted.

One morning, Alex was in two dogfights within ten

minutes and came home tattered and disreputable. Cindy had a strong feeling that the only answer was to put Alex to sleep. So she walked to the vet's, crying and so upset that she could only use gestures to convey what she wished him to do. He understood, took the little cocker and put him to sleep.

Within forty-eight hours she received my letter telling of Tamara's illness and demise. Cindy had Alex for over a year and a half and, though provoked, she had never considered putting him down. But she had picked up my program, which was reinforced by the fact that I was finally writing to her about it, and even as my letter was on its way she acted it out.

If only people would realize that this is happening daily. We are all living little bits of each other's programs: husbands and wives, parents and children, friends. Sometimes it's only for a moment, as when a mother is angry and her child returns the anger. We see married couples who live each other's programs for fifty years. That's why people say that couples of long standing look alike. They *are* alike, through the exchanged vibrations of many years.

People who are sensitive and open may become caught up with a group lacking moral scruples and soon play out their programs. They may then commit robbery, murder, or some other terrible crime. Yet, encountered singly, each is often a fine, perceptive person who failed to recognize whose program it was and ended up believing that he or she really wanted to do what the rest were doing. One person can turn a crowd into a lynch mob simply by being a strong broadcaster whose program drowns out all the others. When the followers are through and the deed is done, they wonder why they ever did it. The Jonestown massacre might well have been such an incident, and I believe that Patricia Hearst was the victim of being sensitive and open to other people's programs.

The beautiful intuitiveness that leads us to feel compassion for others, that can be so constructive when utilized by doctors, counselors and social workers in the service of others, can also be destructive to us when it leads us to carry out programs that are not our own.

PHYSICAL RECEIVING

Physical receiving can be a pain—literally. You can have your Uncle George's headache, your son William's sore shoulder, and even your husband's appendicitis.

I went to the doctor after several days of stomach pain, knowing this wasn't normal for me and something must be wrong. He watched me for a few days, and still couldn't find the source of the pain, so I was put into the hospital for tests. When nothing turned up and the pain persisted, they decided to perform exploratory surgery. The result was negative: nothing organically wrong. After the surgery I talked on the telephone to my husband, from whom I was separated. He was living on another base and I was at my home in Virginia. He told me that he was feeling very upset about the separation, so upset in fact that he had been having recurring stomach pains for days . . .

I realized they had operated on me for his pains. There has to be a limit to togetherness.

My children have teased me so much about my physical empathy and the questing, since the operation, after its source before I will consider it mine, that they have sworn to put this epitaph on my tombstone: *She's not really dead, she's just picking up someone else's condition.* And who knows, they may be right.

I told one mother that her child was an extremely high receiver, right up at the top of the scale. My hope was that she would understand this and not repress or discourage it in any way. To reinforce my opinion, I set up a simple demonstration. I placed seven different colored pens on my desk. I took each top off and then put them in a large envelope where the child couldn't see them. Then I reached my hand into the envelope and held each top, asking the little girl to match what I held, unseen by her, with the correct pen on my desk. She was one hundred percent accurate—at age four.

A year passed and the child was brought to me again. She had developed stomach pains, to the point of having to be taken to the doctor. He was, fortunately, one of those enlightened souls who check all levels, and he looked into her nutrition. Changes in that area resulted in only partial success. When I saw her, I again stressed her extreme sensitivity. I said that we had to consider this in her physical health as well as her nutrition. I checked the child psychically and found nothing wrong with the organs or glands except for the adrenals and digestive-assimilative system. These were running overtime and completely exhausting themselves. To me that indicated the need for a search to find whose program she was getting that could reflect itself in a stomachache. I started with the family.

Her seventeen-year-old brother was not only on drugs, but also dealing them, and therefore under tremendous tension as well as increased sensitivity from their use. He and the little girl were very close, so this program was bouncing back and forth between them like a rubber ball. That would have been enough to produce her stomach pains. But there were an older sister and brother living in the house who were the mother's children from a previous marriage. Their father had suddenly died from a heart attack the week before. This created tremendous upheaval as the mother pitched in and helped them arrange the funeral, since there was no one else to help them. She even had to leave for three or four days to find a military cemetery and attend the burial. She and the two oldest children had gone through a lot of turmoil and the four-year-old was soaking it up.

Her father, the mother's present husband, was vastly irritated about the whole thing. In addition, he was having troubles with his job and with other family connections. He was heading for intestinal problems too, because that was where he buried all his emotions. His reaction to the world was always gut-level (literally).

In the middle of all this was the little girl. Yet they wondered why she had stomachaches. As far as the family was concerned, she wasn't connected with any of it. It was her father's job, her brother's tension, and her mother's and stepbrother's and stepsister's worry about the funeral. There were no words or actions in which the girl had to be involved, but there was a great deal for her to cope with on a psychic level. She was such a receiver that she couldn't help it.

My advice to the mother was to try the blue room, the milk and the protein powder, all meant to induce a slowing-down process. I suggested that they set up these conditions before she took a nap, before bed and, since she had trouble with eating and stomachaches, before she came to the table at mealtimes. It wasn't so unusual for her stomach to ache around that time because that was when she would be with all the family members and their troubles. The child improved markedly under this regime.

Another child had such trouble with her digestive-assimilative system that she could not utilize enough food for proper growth. She was referred to me by her own physician in an effort to increase his own information. (I wish to make it very clear that I did this work in conjunction with the physician; I gave him the information and he used it medically.)

The surprising aspect of this child's condition was that it began when she was still in her mother's womb. I felt it was important, therefore, to know what kind of pregnancy her mother had experienced. As it turned out, it was rather bad. The father didn't want the child and was irritable. The mother felt guilty because she was carrying the source of his anger, yet still she desired the baby. During her pregnancy she was in a severe hypoglycemic state (suffering from low blood sugar). The baby felt all those vibrations because her body was connected to her mother's, and she was born with a less-than-healthy digestive system, but it could be corrected and strengthened now that it was recognized.

At this point, the father said "Well then, it's all my fault!" I could not very well dispute it. Here he was, taking such time and pains to restore his little girl's health, when it was the emotional conditions he set up during his wife's pregnancy that caused the trouble in the first place. The mother said she had been able to sense it even when he had not done or said anything. The baby couldn't hear any words or see any actions, but her solar plexus had picked up the program and was now manifesting a physical reaction.

Some very good books have been written by a well-known psychic in England, Joan Grant.* Her husband is a psychiatrist with a deep interest in our communication levels. She gives many documented cases of hypnosis where he has regressed people to the period of conception and pregnancy. They talk about distaste for the medicine their mothers would take, the feeling of happiness or discord in the home, whether the parents cared for each other or not, and if the pregnancy was wanted. The findings were verified with the parents to see how accurate they were. They found out that the patients could remember the response to things in their bodies even though they could not understand words or actions.

One gynecologist and obstetrician whom I know, is also a hypnotist. When he notices during a delivery that there is undue tension, or that negative things are said out of stress, he makes a note on the mother's chart for her to bring the child in a few years later to be regressed and reprogrammed to eliminate the negative memories of birth.

Many Lifetimes, Far Memory, and others by Joan Grant.

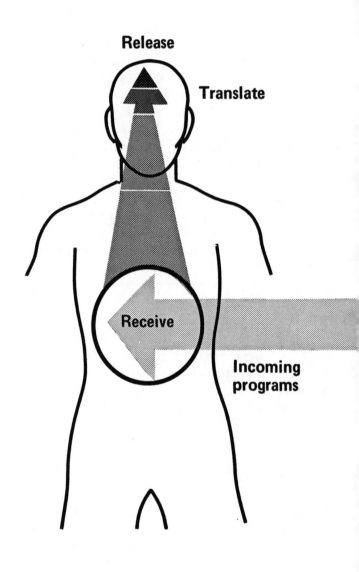

PSYCHIC

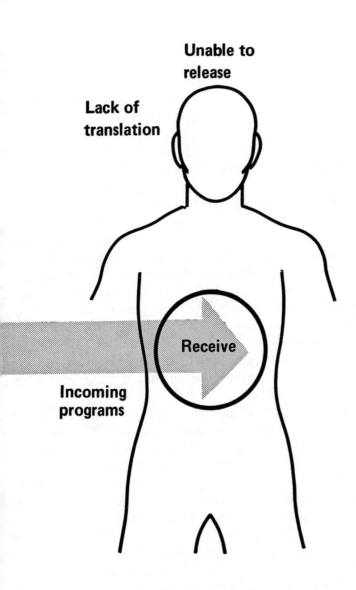

Unable to release

Lack of translation

Receive

Incoming programs

NON·PSYCHIC

93

TRANSLATING

The critical point is between your reception and your translation. The danger lies in not wanting to face what you have received, but trying to color it, distort it, or blank it out. You may fail to investigate every bit of what you receive and leave something out, perhaps the part you don't like. You must practice being an objective observer of the subjective material coming through, insofar as it is humanly possible.

When I was the owner of a modeling school and taught a fashion course, I used to have a point system so that we would be able to tell if someone was overdressed or underdressed. I'd say "Don't tell me that a woman was wearing a blue suit. I want you to tell me that she had on a blue suit composed of three pieces, with four buttons down the jacket, double pleats in the back, and white piping on the cuffs. Give me detail, every detail that you can recall. Don't tell me she wore a gold bracelet, but a gold bracelet set with six assorted stones and a safety chain hanging from it." Everything the eye could see was a point.

We must count off our psychic messages in much the same way. Don't say "I feel hate." Instead say "I feel hate coming from that person and it stems from his dislike of me (or his job, or his marriage, or just that particular day)." Don't look at someone and say they're unhappy. Say they are unhappy because their marriage is on the rocks, financial problems loom, or a child is sick. Particularize.

Don't just go to your solar plexus and say that you feel unhappy, but *why* you feel unhappy.

In the beginning you won't be able to do this. You'll be lucky to know that one person feels positive and another feels negative to you. Soon you will be able to say what kind of positive or negative. You will get a little more each time you work with it.

Often when you are trying to translate information you have received, you will find yourself falling back on your own experiences. This is perfectly normal because we cannot equate anything which we have not experienced in some form or at some level. The person who gets the emotion of happiness may say "It feels just the way I did when I had a hole-in-one" if she's a golfer, or "I feel just the way I did when I closed that big deal last year" if business is her thing. You might have other incidents of happiness that would more closely relate to the situation. Just don't push them out of your mind, thinking "What does that part of my life have to do with it?" Look first and see if you are receiving a symbol to apply to this new situation.

This does not mean you should assume anything. Look at the pictures and feelings you receive, but don't try putting them together through your conscious mind. It is tempting to deliver a pat answer with all the details filled in. But unless you are truly feeling every bit of it, leave the frills alone and fashion a rough but accurate answer.

One well-known psychic in Virginia Beach cut her counseling time down to fifteen minutes per client. I don't believe you can accomplish much in such a short time. It's as if a doctor were to say he is going to take only fifteen minutes with each patient. That may work fine for some, but others will have complications that require looking into and will need more time. In this case, the psychic allowed her time restriction to influence her answers. She jumped to conclusions, she assumed too much, and it had very uncomfortable consequences for one person whom she was counseling.

The nephew of this client came to see me. His aunt, who was unknown to me, had been told by this psychic "I see your nephew . . . I see him with a car accident. I see him being killed. It will be within a period of two years." The aunt had relayed this information to her nephew. Naturally he was quite disturbed when he came to me for counseling. Yet two points came up in our session that led me to a different conclusion. The first was that I could see him living to be quite an old man. The second was that I saw death around him. He told me that his best friend had just been killed in a car accident. In fact, the funeral had been only the day before. When we finished the counseling, he seemed pleased, but asked if I would double-check his lifespan. I did, and thoroughly. I still saw him with many more years to go. That's when he told me the rest of the story about him and the fifteen-minute psychic counselor.

I new this psychic personally and had worked with her. I also knew she was becoming less accurate, though I had never stopped to question why. In order to do her justice, I fed her information through my own solar plexus, exploring it and computing it. She had given his aunt the number *two*. It is easy to get a number in relation to time, but which time? Hours, months, years, what? Past or future? If the timing in a situation is critical, I look for reference points: the foliage of the plants and trees, the ages of the children involved, the feel of a season. It is difficult to pinpoint time and can be a long process, usually taking somewhat longer than fifteen minutes. I then understood how she could have assumed that the *two* meant two years. I asked how long it had been since his aunt had seen her. The answer: two months. That's when I knew what had happened. This psychic had received a *two*, the image of this young man, a car accident and a death, and had added it up to mean his death. She didn't stop to see if he was really in the car accident, or whether it was just around him. She didn't take the time to completely translate, and thus sent the aunt home with misinformation.

All the facts were true. There was an accident and a young man was killed in it, two *months* later. She was a good psychic, but she was shortchanging herself and her clients in the translation process. When I receive something so crucial, I take the time to place the person in the accident and see if he stays dead or remains alive. If he remains alive, obviously he can't be the victim.

Another client asked me if her sister's husband would return alive from Vietnam: a grave question. I had to make sure that my answer was as accurate as possible. Psychically, I put him on the plane and flew him over to Vietnam. Then I saw a military plane explode in mid-air. Having learned my lesson about assuming anything, I said nothing to my client about this crash until I checked further. I took my soldier off the plane in Vietnam and flew him back home. There his family met him at the airport. But still that mid-air explosion remained in my vision.

I asked if he had ever been to Vietnam before, and she said yes. So I plunged in again to see if I was picking up circumstances around his first trip. I placed him back on a plane, flew him over, brought him back, and described the people meeting him when he arrived home: his wife, two children, and a baby. This confirmed that I was seeing his second trip because his wife was still carrying that baby; it had not been born yet. Now that I felt certain of his safe return, I told my client what I had seen that worried me—the military plane exploding in mid-air. She left, and within the hour I received a phone call informing me of the death of an aviator friend and his co-pilot. They had exploded at treetop level over the military base nearby.

So while I was in the vibration of military transportation, I had tuned in on this crash which had nothing to do with my client. If I had not taken the extra ten minutes to check and re-check, I would have thought that he was going to die in that explosion, and I would have been afraid to say that he was coming back alive. I also might have checked out only his first trip if I had assumed it was the present one. That would have been wrong, too. So there is tremendous importance in the way we translate what we receive. It should not be done in a slipshod manner, never taken lightly.

In yet another case, while sitting with a man in my office, I suddenly found myself looking over the shoulder of a young boy. He was on a street corner, watching two ambulance attendants carry a body on a stretcher. I could have told the man nothing but that, and it would have been true as far as it went. But I decided that I must take it further. First I described the boy, but he didn't know a child like that. I told him about the ambulance, and that it was not an ordinary hospital ambulance, but a fire-department or emergency-rescue type. Although I couldn't see the features of the body they were carrying, I knew that it was a man, and that he would be dead before they reached the hospital. Then I corrected myself, for I realized that he was already dead. He had died instantly.

All of this came through like a news broadcast, and I was so totally caught up in it that I had to carry it through to the end. I said there was cement connected with it. I watched the child as the body was placed in the ambulance, thinking perhaps he was the connection, but he turned and walked down the street. I stopped and looked at my office clock, noting the exact time. Since my client had no apparent connection with these things, I tried to place it in my own life. I believed at that time that anything coming through while I counseled was pertinent to myself or my client. But I reached no solution either way.

That evening, I mentioned it to my family. The next morning my daughter came in with the newspaper, saying "Mother, here's your experience." There on the front page was an article about a fire marshal inspecting a building. The building had a conveyor belt carrying bags of cement from the lower to the upper floor. Instead of using the stairs, the inspector hopped a ride on the conveyor, but he got caught on it, his head was crushed and he died instantly. Since he was a fire marshal, the department used one of their own vehicles instead of a hospital ambulance. The accident occurred as I was looking at my office clock, precisely.

This was a tremendous learning experience for me. I found that I should never lock myself into a pattern built merely on experiences; that I should be open to all sorts of possibilities in this field. I can receive programs that have nothing to do with me or the person with me. As a radio, I am open to all sorts of airwaves, including the quick, seemingly unrelated newsflash.

As it happened, this was not a random transmission. Six weeks later a woman called my office for an appointment. She was the fire marshal's widow. Because of my experience, I was able to give her knowledge and comfort.

Children rarely distort intuitions. The four-year-old I mentioned earlier predicted snow in Sacramento, California, and it snowed for the first time in years. She hadn't been taught to distort her reception with conscious thought; it was still pure. She didn't know that conditions in Sacramento are supposed to make snow an impossibility. She just knew that it was going to snow.

We must be the same. It is easy to pick what we want to happen or what the other person wants to hear. It took me a long time to weed out others' conscious thoughts and desires and what they wanted me to see. Many times I've told clients various things and they've said "That's impossible. All the facts are here. It can't turn out that way." But it has. They could have told the little girl that snow was impossible in Sacramento. They could have convinced her that her subconscious must be wrong. And they would have felt very silly as they stood in the falling snowflakes.

An author named John Evans says "Listen with your soul instead of your mind. Your soul hears with eternal wisdom; your mind is a product of conditioning and time." That sums it up for me.

If you are going to do it properly, stick to the truth of it. If you can't get anything more than "I don't feel good around that person," at least accept that. Don't try to make it anything more. There is more out there, but don't worry if you don't get it in the beginning. Simply stick to the part that's true and the rest will come with practice.

These last few examples have been controlled situations of receiving while counseling. At that time you are aware of other programs and deliberately picking out who is who and what is what and tracking information as far as you can to get the entire picture accurately. But reception doesn't stop there; it follows us everywhere and in everything we do. And so must our translator.

From my own experience, I can say it is very easy to fall into the trap of playing out others' programs if we receive them and fail to translate them properly. A good example of this concerns the mother of a young woman my son was dating in Virginia. I had never met her, but on one particular occasion I stopped by her house. It was a beautiful day, warm and sunny, and I felt marvelous. I went to the door and rang the bell. There was no answer. The car was in the driveway, so I reasoned that someone was home and rang the bell again. Still there was no response, so I gave it a final try. I was becoming extremely angry with this woman, really disliking her, when suddenly I stopped and let my translator take over.

Until now I had felt as beautiful as the day. Furthermore, I had never even met the woman. Under these circumstances, why was I becoming so angry and disliking her so? Then it became clear. I recalled my son had said that the woman worked nights and therefore had to sleep late during the days. So she was in her bedroom trying to rest, while I was leaning on her doorbell, no doubt really irritating her. It was nothing personal (there was no way she could know it was me), she just wished whoever it was would stop ringing and go away. I had been picking up that anger and wearing it like a coat—someone else's coat. When I translated that, and understood it, then I could release the anger and walk away feeling like myself again. And let the lady, whom I no longer disliked, go back to sleep.

RELEASING

After we acknowledge and translate our information, then we can release it. This is so simple, yet so complicated. If I were to sum it up, I would say that *knowledge is release.* If you place someone in a strange dark room, they will be afraid. If you turn the lights on and let them have a look before you darken it, they will be all right. They will know what is there, even if they can't see it, and they will release their fear. When we do not identify our programs, we are bound by fear of the unknown.

If we are "getting" something, and we don't know what, or where it's from, we must bring it all the way through and look at it in the light; then we are no longer under its control. We can cope with it and, by knowledge and recognition, release it.

If I go around all day with an uncomfortable feeling in the pit of my stomach, the only way to release it is to sit down and find out where it is originating. If I do, I find that it leaves me. If I pick up your program and call you on the telephone, and you acknowledge it is yours, then it will leave me. If I think about who it might be and I hit the right person, it will go away. It helps to remember who it was and when it stopped, just in case you get it again. Eliminate your suspects!

Some people maintain that I, as a counselor, should correct programs for my clients. But I believe we are all at that stage of civilization where responsibility for self must be developed to the fullest. It is your discomfort, and it is up to you to take steps toward releasing it. If you wish to ask me for help, then I will join you in the responsibility, but you must still take that first step of seeking help. It would not help you if I did the whole thing for you, because then you wouldn't learn how to handle the problem so that it does not occur again.

If we sit in a hole expecting someone to come along and dig us out of it, that is not accepting responsibility for ourselves. Believe me, it could be a long wait.

You people who go around helping people out of holes have a responsibility too. To yourself. It took me a long time to learn that. As a natural humanitarian, I would help any-

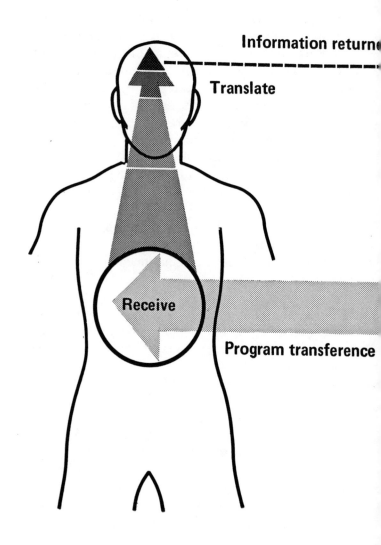

Information return

Translate

Receive

Program transference

PSYCHIC COUNSELOR

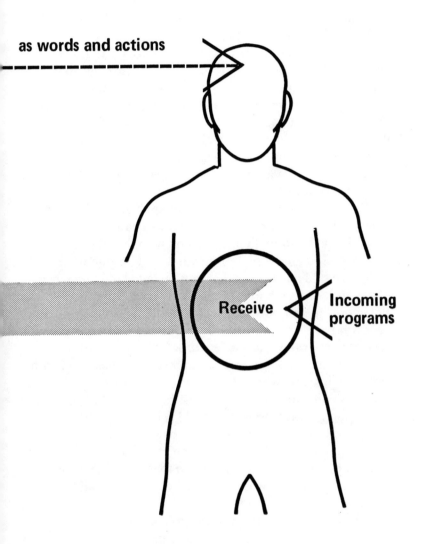

CLIENT

one who needed help . I was always to be found championing the underdog. That resulted in some unhappy situations because some people really didn't want help, or didn't want to be indebted for help, or refused to acknowledge that they needed help at all. I would rush out to help the underdog, only to find he often bit, and that upset me. I was like the Boy Scout in the cartoon who is trying to help the old lady across the street when she doesn't want to go, and I couldn't understand when she didn't appreciate my dragging her across. I learned the hard way that I cannot help anyone who doesn't want to help himself.

Gradually I found my method changing. Just how much, I realized at a party one night. A woman came into the room and told me I had to go upstairs and help this poor man who was confused and upset. Immediately I inquired "Did he ask?" She said no, so I told her that I would help him when he came and asked me and not before. Her asking for him did not count. After I had done it, I thought, "This is coming out of my mouth? The person who used to run around cramming help down various and sundry throats?"

It is like giving someone a tool before he has reached the point in his life where he knows how to use it. I've had mothers come and say "You must help me with this child!" One "child" was thirty-three and I repeated the advice I had given the woman who asked me to help the man at the party. If he wanted help, he would come to me and I would help him. But he had to be willing to do that much. Otherwise all my effort would be wasted. So, all you helpers out there . . . release!

The release mechanism is so simple, yet people make it so complicated that we have to go into detail to explain its very simplicity. Release is nothing more than acknowledging and understanding on a conscious level what it is that's come through, where it goes and what has caused it.

ON/OFF BUTTON

Once you get the knack of releasing what you don't want, you can shut down your powerhouse at will. Often people do not realize this and, when they meet me socially, expect that I see their lives spread out before me like an open book. When I am not working with a client I am content to accept people for whatever role they choose to play, or see whatever aspect they wish to present to me. I don't want to spend my life working twenty-four hours a day. When I go to visit someone at the hospital, I tune out the programs around me. Otherwise a great deal of pain and suffering would come through my being. I have the ability to tune in the programs I choose.

The humorous side of this is that some people are afraid to be around me for fear I will see the skeletons in their closets. When I was a novice, they occasionally had reason to fear that from me. One time I turned to the woman next to me and confided, "That man over there is cheating on his wife . . . (giggle, giggle)." Guess who the man's wife was?

Discretion is learned, one way or another. There is much to be said for turning your button to off at a party and now I always do.

The next time you get cornered by a curiosity seeker who is simply fascinated by the psychic world, tell him you are switched to off and intend to stay there for the rest of the party. Then broadcast your own programs and prepare to meet the most fascinating people there.

NINE
Commercial and Foreign Stations

There is a restaurant in a nearby town where I always feel welcome and happy. It is small and unpretentious, but it has been tastefully decorated in a natural way and the people who work there thoroughly enjoy what they are doing. The owner has attracted to his staff creative people who need to make a living, and he allows them to work out their own hours. The food is all fresh, and there is excitement over devising new recipes, which they do all the time. Everyone in the restaurant feels a part of its success, and you can feel those "good vibes" when you walk through the door.

Contrast this with the atmosphere of a famous restaurant in a major American city. There you will find French food and hordes of waiters working in a building of historical importance. Obviously trading on their famous name and the plentiful supply of tourists, they have forsaken hospitality for unbridled rudeness. On one occasion, a hapless guest was served a portion of creamed peas instead of the requested hors d'oeuvres and, being famished, began to eat them. A moment later, a different waiter skidded to a halt by the table and snatched the dish from under the startled diner's nose, screaming "*What* are you eating?" As if that weren't enough, he then called the other waiter to account on the spot, and everyone at the table was treated to a very nasty scene. The vibrations in that restaurant are so negative that dining there is a tension-filled experience you are unlikely to repeat.

Good vibrations are good business. Make no mistake about it, vibrations may be intangible, but they are real. Vibrations are given off by individuals (as they broadcast), but they are also given off by groups—in homes, businesses, cities, states, and nations. All have their unique vibrations.

An orthodontist once sent his entire staff to me so they could learn how their vibrations affected the patients. Each individual—dentist, technician, receptionist—broadcasted a program to the patient, and there was another vibration of the total working unit. I explained that if they brought negative programs to work, they would change the vibration and the flow of the entire office. But if they came to work in a positive frame of mind, they would literally draw people to them, and business would prosper.

Owners of businesses spend a great deal of time and money on location, architecture and interior design, hoping to produce a desirable effect. They should continue the job by paying attention to the vibrations of each part of the enterprise. What colors are they using? Are they screening their staff to find positive personal vibrations as well as business qualifications? (How many people will return to a shop or restaurant where the salesperson or the waiter has been surly or indifferent?) If you want a successful business, every program coming from it should be monitored to make sure it is in harmony.

I believe it is only sensible to consider its vibration as you create your product. How much more desirable it will be if it is lovingly crafted to be the very best of its kind! Customers may not be able to say why they prefer your product, but they will unconsciously respond to its natural vibration. If the product is harmonious, it will resonate for them. Some people say that, when they go shopping, certain things "hum" for them. This is not just a way of speaking. It describes the reality that certain objects—clothes, food, whatever—are just right for certain people. I think that when you are in a shop and you have that feeling about something, you should buy it.

How often will you buy something because it is popular at the moment, or because the salesperson says "Oh, you look adooorable in that!" and then go home and never use it. You can learn to get in touch with your feelings and know whether something really feels right for you. In a bookstore I will carry a book around the shop with me until I either want to put it back or take it to the cashier. Inevitably when I take it home there is something in it that is valuable to me.

Some years ago, when we were stationed near Kamakura, Japan, I went shopping with another Navy wife. As we strolled along, I spotted in an antique shop window a bronze figure that strangely appealed to me. My friend said "That's Hotei, he's the god of happiness." Indeed, the figure of the baldheaded little fat man wore a wide smile. There was something about him that I loved instantly, though I had never been particularly interested in statues. Then I shook my head, reminding myself that I had promised my husband not to accumulate a lot of junk that would not be used when we returned home. So my friend and I had lunch and drove back to the base. All the way home I kept wishing that I had gone back to the shop one more time.

The next time I went to Kamakura I returned to the shop, taking my friend to interpret for me. Hotei was still there, but the price was much more than I felt comfortable about paying. Again we went to lunch, but I couldn't wait to go back and buy him, which I did. Hotei sat in a prominent place on my Japanese coffee table and was the object of much teasing by Navy personnel.

Back home in the States, Hotei resumed his place on the

table. This was the time when I first started seeking out psychics, and all of them described a fat, baldheaded man around me. No one in my life fit that description. One day I was seated on my sofa in meditation and I glanced over at Hotei who, I suddenly realized, was the little man everyone had seen. I ran to my storage closet and rummaged through the things from Japan until I found a book about the gods of the Orient which I had purchased but never read. Why would Hotei be around me? After all, he was just a statue.

I found to my surprise that Hotei was the only one of the seven gods who was a mortal. He had been a Zen priest, wandering the countryside, making prophesies with great accuracy, but only for those who believed in it. He was known in the Orient as the god of prophecy and of fortune tellers. No wonder I was drawn to him! And he to me.

Kamakura is the ancient capital of Japan, and it is a place with the most profound vibrations. A gigantic statue of Buddha draws thousands of visitors to the temple there, and one cannot fail to notice the beautiful vibrations around that statue. You can sense all the people who have sat in contemplation over the hundreds of years of its existence. It is incredibly peaceful.

Places accumulate the vibrations of all those who have been there and the events in which they participated. A similar feeling pervades the cliff dwellings at Mesa Verde in the American Southwest.

My father went back to ranching in New Mexico some years ago. The main ranchhouse on his spread was the old Fort Apache. There were soldiers buried up on the knoll. I understood there was an Indian chief buried near the horse corrals. That area of the ranch gave off some vibes. But my father decided to build a new ranchhouse back in a box canyon much further into the 56,000 acres of land. I could sit there in that place and sense Indians pouring down into the canyon. It turned out that this was where Geronimo had had his last hideout. Very little occurred at that place since then, and the vibrations were still quite clear.

Nobody can walk the streets of Colonial Williamsburg and not have a sense of what happened there. You can virtually see the colonists walking down the streets. A visit to the cemetery gives one the feeling of being surrounded by all those early Americans.

When I flew into Belfast, Ireland, about five years ago to visit my daughter, I was aware of such dense negativity that it was hard to believe. It was like a heavy blanket, suffocating in its effect. The three weeks I spent there were weighed down by the weary war and the emotions of the people around me. There were bombings and shootings, and the city looked like a World War II movie set, complete with barbed wire blockades, demolished cars and buses left lying in the roads.

In the butcher shop, I found myself nervously checking to see if anyone carried a bomb. On the TV came sporadic announcements asking that anyone having information on a certain situation call a number and report it. Or, shopkeepers were warned to go to their shops because there was word that a fire bomb was about to go off. If we went out to dinner, we were admitted to the restaurant and the door was locked behind us.

I saw that the people had become resigned, and somehow immune, to this existence. A local doctor told me that if the war stopped, everyone would need psychiatric care. They would not know how to live without the tremendous pressure under which they now labored. The relief would leave them apathetic and helpless.

I did not realize the extent to which I had acclimatized myself to this state of seige until my plane took off. As we left the ground at Belfast I could feel the heaviness dropping away. We were leaving it behind.

Flying towards the North American continent, I became

aware that even continents have their characteristic vibrations, and that they are detectable from the air. Coming in to
Washington and the Virginia countryside that I love so
much, I had a wonderful sense of the familiar and it felt very
good to me.

Another time I felt that familiarity was my very first visit
to London. There was just something about London that I
knew. But the feeling was not as strong as when I visited
Cornwall in the southwest corner of England. When I arrived
in the tiny Cornish town of St. Ives, I felt as if I'd always been
there. I drank my beer in a 1200-year-old pub and lived in a
castle. Local families told me they couldn't believe the way
the town had taken to me. Normally they hold themselves
remote from strangers, but they loved me instantly and I felt
the same about them. It was extraordinary.

I do think it is true that you will be accepted anywhere if
you really expect to enjoy yourself. That positive anticipation
is always picked up by the local people and reciprocated. I
have made about forty moves and I have yet to live in a place
that I didn't find acceptance and feel right at home.

In Kamakura there was a restaurant to which Americans
never went because the owner had lost three sons in World
War II. But I went there and showed them how much I en-
joyed them, and they forgot our national differences. The
positive vibration you send out is irresistible. People respond
in kind.

As pebbles in a pond, the rings of our vibrations ripple out
to encompass our towns and states. If a city is full of negativity and upheaval, you can feel this when you drive into it. The
gambling cities of Nevada emit unique vibrations. When I
play blackjack or shoot craps, I pick up all the feelings of the
other people present. That blows any hopes I may have of a
surefire, psychically conceived winning streak. You have to
be a pillar of objectivity to shut off all those other programs.
Some people are having a good time because they have the

money to do it, while others are frightened and desperate. There have been occasions when I could rise above all that and get lucky, but it is enormously difficult. Perhaps the compulsive gambling that puts so many people in the casinos is simply the result of some eager money-chaser's program being perpetually played out.

Passing through Big Sur on my way to a conference in Santa Barbara one day, I suddenly turned to the driver and asked if he was playing games in his head. He assured me he was not, but I still had this games image. A few minutes later he asked me where Esalen Institute was, and I noted that we were approaching it. The game-playing vibration increased as we passed Esalen and I pointed it out to my friend. No sooner had we passed it than the feeling began to diminish, until it faded all together. When I mentioned it to my conference group of therapists and professionals, they burst into laughter. I had been unconsciously responding to what was going on at Esalen. They said they could identify with that reaction completely.

Personal vibrations are very potent in people's homes. A home embodies the total essence of your family—what it is, what it feels, and what it has experienced. You can tell a lot about a person by walking into his or her house, and it is more than the furniture arrangement, wallpaper or rugs from which you get the information. Children are adept at picking up whether it is a house filled with love or with hate. Probably you remember both kinds of houses from your own childhood. Plants will thrive in a happy home and languish and die where the vibrations are negative. Sometimes I meet a family where all the members seem to be sunny and positive; other families have a uniformly sour view of life. Both are quite contagious.

When someone is tense and reluctant to have guests in the house, those guests are going to have a hard time relaxing. On the other hand, the happy host may have difficulty in getting his guests to leave! A home reflects quite precisely how people feel about themselves. If they are in balance, their homes will resonate in a most attractive manner.

One final vibration I want to mention here is prayer. I believe that prayer is the projecting of positive feelings toward a particular person or thing. The words or the structure are simply the vehicles for the positive vibrations being sent forth. The prayer of one person can be extremely strong. When many people join together in prayer, an abundance of positive energy envelops the object of that prayer. We can certainly use more of that.

TEN
Meditation

Multiple choice is my favorite type of quiz because there is a good chance of getting the answer right the first time. Now, which of the following people are meditating?

1. A housewife doing dishes.
2. A driver at a red light.
3. A teenager putting on her makeup.
4. A guru sitting in the lotus position with a bowl on his lap.

Time's up. The answer: Everyone but the guru—he's having his lunch. Yes, the others really are meditating. Meditation is such a simple thing, yet we often seem to foul it up by making it out to be more than it is.

When I first learned to use meditation, I had to be without distractions to sustain it. While my husband was at sea, I was almost smug about my ease with it. Then he came home and we had an argument and it shot my whole psychic ability to pieces. One snarl in the morning and my counseling was finished for the day. I had to learn to detach myself from personal pain in order to reach the necessary level of awareness.

Even when that was resolved, there were other distractions: Four children and various animals do not tiptoe around the house. Coping with assorted barkings, squabblings, rock music, slammed doors, continual phone calls and first-aid advice, even a fulltime mother and housekeeper could have been driven mad, let alone a psychic counselor who needed a delicate balance of introspection for her work. On the other hand, maybe my developing the ability to withdraw saved my sanity. Gradually I trained myself to reach high levels of concentration despite all these interferences. It strengthened me and taught me a lot about the nature of meditation.

There are those who find that they can use this detachment on a permanent basis as an exit from life. It feels so good for them to leave their worries below and behind them that they decide to try for an all-time high. It is a way of avoiding responsibility. They get to the point where they are spending more and more time in the meditative state, not because of the awareness it offers, but because they can thereby avoid facing their problems on this plane of existence.

I watched a group in Virginia Beach do this; they were getting further and further removed from physical reality with each passing minute. Finally I told one member that I thought her life on the conscious plane was one of the biggest messes in the world. She was sitting there telling me about all the wonderful things "out there," and I wondered what good it was to her if it couldn't be used to enhance her everyday living. As long as you are in physical manifestation, you'd better learn to live in balance here. And come down from there when I am talking to you!

I often come into conflict with people who maintain that you cannot be on the spiritual path and also have the pleasures of this world. Rubbish. If I am, in fact, part of the God force, along with all those objects and beings on this earth, then I am not going against God if I: love other human beings, have sex, sit down to dinner, know the pleasure of a home, furniture, clothing, and transportation. What makes me happy makes the God within me happy, too.

There is also much confusion and disapproval among these people about my making a living from something that they feel is a gift from God. I've seen psychics live in squalor and destitution because they believe it is wrong to make any money out of this "gift." Many people are talented artists, and surely that is another gift from God, yet no one sees the harm in their feeding and clothing themselves by selling a canvas. I can see no difference between the two.

I've seen many people allow their children to run around without proper housing, clothing or security while they are doing "God's work." All I can say is, "Remember, those children are God's work, too." The common phrase "I'm going to do my own thing" has covered some of the greatest shirking of responsibility in the world. Balance is a difficult thing to achieve. When I think that I have one area of my life worked out, something else always comes along that needs attention. This is a working existence, always needing constant adjustment to maintain an even keel. There are many times when I would like to just float away, too.

Recently a man told me that I should never get married. Had he known that I've been married twice already, he might have had some foundation for his remark. But his reason was that I was so *evolved* that I should keep my attention on higher things, and away from carnal desires. I told him that if I elected to come to this physical world with a physical body and all its needs, then I would be just as wrong to starve it from sexual love as I would be to starve it from food. To me, the body is made to react and have needs, and there is nothing wrong in meeting those needs.

I have heard some people say that they think it is wonderful that they are abstaining from physical relationships. Or they describe a past incarnation as a priest or priestess where they abstained from personal contact, thinking that it means they have reached a high level of spiritual development to have lived like that. Maybe. My own thinking on this subject is that it is a piece of angel cake to achieve the lofty realms of consciousness through meditation in a life where you don't have to think about your food, clothing, shelter, transportation or the woes of this world. All you have to do is continually pray or meditate. I'm not saying that such a life is worthless or in error. I'm simply saying that such a person does not have the worries that we have who are in the world and of the world.

I must do my work each day in a meditative state and still worry about food for myself and my family, college for my children, rent, electricity, water, garbage, the oil leak in the car, the whole package. I have to do this and still strive for the path of spiritual awareness. Give me a person who can resolve all those problems and still sit next to the Carpenter's Son and I'll admit that he's an advanced student.

As to meditation classes, I have already mentioned that I am against indiscriminately taught courses that fail to explain all sides to meditation. They will tell you that you are more sensitive and open while practicing meditation, but fail to warn that the programs coming through are not always yours, nor are they always desirable or beneficial. Think of the astronauts: If we were to shoot them into space without knowing how to bring them back, it would be of no use to us or to them. We not only have to send them out, but bring them back. Otherwise, all the great knowledge and experience they might gather will not benefit anyone.

A case in point concerns a call I received one beautiful morning at six. My peace was shattered for me by the hysterical voice of a woman calling me from the East Coast. She had been assured that I would know how to help her and wanted an appointment. I looked at my schedule and saw that it would be at least six weeks before I could squeeze her in, and I knew from the sound of her voice that she wouldn't last that long. So I decided to help her over the telephone.

She calmed down enough to tell me that she'd started a course in mind expansion a few weeks before and that strange things had been happening to her ever since. She had asked her class instructor about them, only to be told that there couldn't possibly be any connection between her experiences and the course. She was on the verge of a nervous breakdown. It seemed they had taught her that meditation was a stage between waking and sleeping, and suggested that a good time to practice was just before going to sleep. That is when the strange occurrences began. She was unmarried at the time and a Virginia-bred lady, so she had difficulty telling me about it. What it amounted to was that she was having orgasms regularly while meditating. It was scaring her to death.

I asked her if any of the instructors had explained that the course would heighten her state of sensitivity not only mentally and spiritually, but also emotionally and physically. She replied that they really hadn't gone into things like that. I then explained that the instructors should have told her that meditation stimulates all the glands, not just one, and leads, among other things, to an increase in sexual sensitivity.

It was curious though, as to why she was manifesting an overload in that particular area, so I asked her to describe her bedroom. As you may have guessed, it was red. Lovely red florals everywhere. So meditating in that color raised all her sensitivity, but the sex glands particularly were aroused. I recommended the usual can-of-paint routine, and suggested that we check into other areas in her life including her diet, emotional state, and family connections, to see the state she had been in before she began her heightened awareness. This would assure that the woman returned to a balanced condition.

Even the simplest things, like electricity, must be handled with care. We should use it without fear, but certainly with care, never forgetting that such a powerful thing can do us great harm. Things can kill us or heal us, depending on how we use them. Like everything else, the psychic field has a positive and a negative side. Understanding will provide a useable tool. Wrapping ESP in mysticism or magic, those hoary smokescreens, will effectively stifle it.

People are being hoodwinked when they are told that they can *learn* to meditate. To my way of thinking, you cannot learn to meditate. You can only learn to structure your time and your life so that you *will* meditate. I know of one woman who was so busy with children during the day that she went each night to an ashram in a neighboring town to meditate with the people there, even though she was not of their faith. She said that the peace and quiet of the place, and the fact that no one was there asking her to tie a shoelace or settle a fight, taught her to meditate without any lessons.

I have said often in this book that it is the taking of the time to be psychic that counts. You may also learn to relax your body so that you can meditate, and you may learn techniques that will help you reach the meditative state more easily. But other than that, you are already doing it naturally in many ways. Meditation is that minute, hour, day, or whatever, that you spend relaxing the conscious mind and being in touch with the subconscious. The woman who is washing her dishes has done them so often that her mind is anywhere but in the sink. She is meditating. She will suddenly think of someone she hasn't thought of in years and the next day that person will call. She'll say, "Isn't that interesting? I thought of him yesterday while I was doing the dishes and now he's called." She thought of him because her conscious mind didn't have to hang around guiding her thoughts, and her subconscious was free to wander.

The man who drives the same route to work each day, and doesn't realize he's going to work until he is already there, is meditating. He may find an answer that has been eluding him when it just flashes into his mind. He is in an altered state of consciousness.

I do the same thing at a red light. In those seconds before the light turns green, when I have nothing to do and nowhere to go, I'll find that sudden thoughts come to me. I can see this becoming a hazard to the motorists of the world. An arresting officer's dialogue might go something like this:

> "Say, fella, have you been meditating? Let's see your driver's license. Uh-huh. Would you mind getting out and walking this straight line? Why your feet don't even touch the ground! Sorry, Sport, I'm going to have to take you to the station and book you for driving under the influence of meditation. That's a misdemeanor in this state, ya' know."

The fortunate person who has the time to sit down in front of the fire and do nothing but watch it flicker, will find himself taking a fantasy trip. It is a marvelous meditative state. So is kicking off your shoes after a hard day and not thinking about the pile of work on your desk, or raising the kids, or anything.

If this is what meditation is is all about, how can anyone teach us to do it? We achieve it naturally when we don't scare it away by making a big thing of it. All you need to learn is how to get there more often and more easily. Basically, you are already there.

Use anything that works for you. I, myself, would rather sit in front of the fireplace and say "I have an hour off from the rest of the world. I'm going to get in touch with myself and with what is going on." I know that is as good as any class. If you want to develop your psychic mind, then you have to do it the same way you develop your muscles. Take that hour, or at least thirty minutes, each day—and put your natural ability into it.

ELEVEN
A Light Show For Life

Having run the gamut from crystal balls to tarot cards, automatic writing, ouija boards, and self-hypnosis, I find they are all merely tools that are available to us as we increase our sensitivity to the universe. Some of these tools worked better for me than others. It seems that a great deal of personal preference is involved, with people choosing the method that feels most congenial to them. But they all bring the same results. They are the keys that unlock your psychic awareness.

The good card reader is not really divining all those answers from the cards. The cards are used over and over again, yet the message is different for each individual each time. There aren't any movie screens in that crystal ball, either. Believe me, I had severe eyestrain until I realized that I was going about it the wrong way. The crystal ball is just another method for activating the mind's eye. Yoga provides still another method. It relaxes the body and stimulates the glands, putting the practitioner in perfect condition to use the natural meditative abilities.

I reject none of these aids, because they often help release the psychic from his or her conscious mind. You may find it comfortable to use one of these tools, such as cards or crystal, or you may decide to "psych it out" using no aids whatsoever.

I have found a method combining color and tone that is beneficial on many levels to me and to my students. It has the advantage of being instrumental in bringing the centers and their physical counterparts into a state of balance. That balance is a vital step toward achieving psychic sensitivity and awareness. It also acts as a release mechanism for any tension or suppression picked up during the day. Its qualities of relaxation make it invaluable for anyone working under the stresses of today's world. In fact, it has something to offer everyone striving for a healthier, more balanced existence. I will tell you more about it later in the chapter.

THAT OLD RED/ORANGE/YELLOW/GREEN/BLUE/ INDIGO/PURPLE MAGIC

Tibetan Buddhism has long used color to aid in healing, particularly in healing mental illness. They use color in conjunction with size and shape. For instance, within a building used only for that purpose, they will construct wall partitions that can be moved to change the shape, length, height, and breadth of a room. The walls are painted in different colors. For mental problems, a prescription is made concerning the color, size and shape of the room, and the patient is asked to remain in that room for a specified amount of time. The colors and shapes relate to various aspects of Buddhist teaching.

The ancient sun worshippers knew that the sun's rays were beneficial for all types of illness. Modern sun worshippers still experience a sense of well-being from exposure to the sun. Since its rays contain the entire spectrum, it is reasonable to assume that the balance of colors is an important therapeutic factor. In our own times, results have been claimed for a wide variety of healings and readjustments of the body, as well as rebalancing of the mind and emotions, through color therapy.

Color is a form of energy. Think of it not just as visual, but as waves of energy flowing through our bodies, as perceptible to them as X-ray or radio waves. It has been found that color actually penetrates the skin. Accepting this, we can easily see that it affects us as surely as standing under a shower has the effect of getting us wet. The suggestion has recently been made that we receive color's benefits best through our eyes, and therefore glasses, sunglasses, or windowpanes are harmful because they screen the light.

Color therapies have included the wearing of prescribed colors in clothes and gems, and even the consumption of liquids and foods that have been exposed to various colors. These practices are meant to enhance the specific properties of each hue. Scientific and medical research has corroborated these ideas.

MUSIC: COLOR'S PERFECT MATE

Music is also a form of energy. It comes to us as sound waves which we perceive through hearing. As we all know, it has legendary qualities ranging from soothing "the savage breast" to stirring it up quite a lot. Adolf Hitler was adept in the use of thrilling anthems to play on nationalistic feelings. On a more mundane, though still manipulative, level, supermarkets have found that the livelier the music they play, the faster their customers shop. Almost everyone feels compelled to tap her foot to a lively tune. On the darker side, intense dissonances or shrill tones are known to cause mental disturbance if prolonged. Sounds that are painful to the ear can actually cause physical organs to distort if there is no relief from them. Many people have experienced ultrasound medical treatments for a variety of conditions. There are endless examples of the effects of sound on living organisms, but it is also true that a singer *can* shatter glass if he happens to discover its harmonic vibrations.

Color and sound combined can have a profound effect on our physical, mental and emotional well-being. A claim was made centuries ago for the healing effects experienced by people standing beneath a stained glass window in a church while singing or praying. This was said to restore the feeble and infirm to a more balanced state of health. In the Chapel of St. Louis in Paris, a wall of ancient stained glass bathes visitors in a rainbow of colors, and many comment on the feeling of peace that comes to them.

Closer to home, the disco displays one of the most stimulating combinations of color and sound modern man has produced, though I doubt if the results are totally positive. Strobes or other rapidly flashing lights may cause disorientation, or even an altered state of consciousness. In some cases of brain wave diseases, epileptic seizures may result. Bright, bold patterns assailing the eyes create confusion (as the brief Op Art craze showed), and they can stimulate the body centers in ways that are not necessarily healthy. Loud, heavy, discordant music pulses through the ears and body, laying seige to it willy-nilly.

My particular combinations of color and tone is a little different and unquestionably more beneficent.

Up My Own Rainbow

That there is a consistent pattern to the way color affects us has been revealed to me over years of counseling and research. Hundreds of clients displayed symptoms or had reactions to particular colors so consistently and predictably that I could pinpoint their problem areas just by these responses. It became undeniable. I decided that this was a useful tool and set about to create a practical device for producing colors and tones.

Countless hours were spent consulting with experts in color and lighting—artists, engineers and designers—working in offices, studios, and any other available space. We wanted to be sure to produce the purest possible color and tone, and we struggled to find a design that would be practical and easy to operate. We took photos of color, made color wheels of endless materials, experimented with spotlights, pinlights, and lamp bulbs, anything to achieve the goal of projecting pure color into a room. We even tried dying objects with color, and for a time I would stagger wearily out of someone's laboratory or garage workshop with more color on me than anywhere else. After much experimenting, we decided upon colored slides. The most feasible way to accomplish exposure seemed to be the standard screen and projector.

I then took my idea to a professional sound studio, where the colors were matched scientifically with their proper musical tones. The whole project began to shape up. I used the colors and tones in my classes and at home for myself and my family. But the necessity for the bulky screen and projector became more and more of a drawback.

Two more years of design work (in which my son, Bill Rink, participated as an electrical engineer with a psychic orientation) culminated in the production of the *Kaleidacolor*,* a beautiful globe of light with remote control that can manifest the benefits of color and tone anywhere. Its size allows it to be used anywhere with a minimum of fuss. It can be used on an office desk, in a study or bedroom, in the classroom, a therapist's office, or a doctor's waiting room with a maximum of results.

---

*The *Kaleidacolor* may be obtained by writing to Kaleidacolor, Cupertino, California 95014. This company also manufactures associated products for classroom and individual use. It continues to research and produce aids for extrasensory perception and its development.

TUNING UP

You know that each gland has a corresponding color and musical note. Think of the glands as a piano, one gland to each key. If a single key is out of tune, the whole song is going to sound off-key. Before a performance, you normally tune the piano. Before you use the body, you should tune all the glands in the same manner. Overuse of a particular color will overstimulate the gland with which it is associated. Underuse will do just the opposite. If a gland has been suppressed in any way for a period of time, there will also be an imbalance. So tuning is necessary to keep your instrument in harmony and acquire health, sensitivity and balance.

If you sit down every day and do the following exercise, it will enhance your ability to reach the meditative state and relax the entire body. To balance your body is to make it well.

First, visualize a color (for instance, red) and the gland with which it is connected. Hold that vibration for a few moments. If that gland has been working on an unhealthy vibratory level, it will start to return to its normal rate and level. With the "Kaleidacolor," of course, you don't need to do the visualization; it does that for you. I normally allot two minutes to each color, but after a hard day, you may feel the need for a longer duration. The corresponding note is automatically played with each color. I recommend that you wear light cotton clothing. Avoid synthetics, for the color will not penetrate as well. If the conditions and temperature permit, wear no clothing at all. Make sure that you are in a relaxed position.

While you look at each color and listen to each note, get in touch with that part of your body to which it is related. Visualize bathing each area and gland with the energies of that color and tone. I'm not asking you to concentrate on anything; that defeats the purpose of the relaxation. Just gently channel your perception to the physical body.

I work from the bottom up, starting with red. Those of

you who have had too much physical activity on any given day, or not enough, will find that your red glands are not functioning properly. If you have resisted hitting someone in the nose, you have changed the vibration of your red. It is the same if you have been chasing children around the house or the classroom. With the colors and tones, you have the opportunity to go back, at least once a day, and restore harmony. Then your body will be able to keep up with you.

Follow the colors all the way from red to purple. That is sufficient for an overall cleaning out of your centers—great before dinner for digestion, or before starting your work day. The whole family can sit through it and begin with a better state of health and attitude.

For a deeper, more effective cleansing and relaxation, you can maintain the color for a longer period or run through them twice. Remember to start with the red and end with the purple.

If you are planning to do a little psychic homework, you will want to descend from the purple, one color at a time, back down to the yellow. (Remember, yellow is your psychic radio, located in your solar plexus.) Only stop at this color when you are planning to work on your psychic ability with the exercises I will give you in the next chapter. After all my emphasis on shutting down this center, now I want you to open it; this is standard procedure in my classes. After you have finished practicing, take the colors back up to purple and stop. This will leave your centers balanced and secure.

For those of you who work so hard that you are too tired to stay up for the process, you can run the colors and tones while you drift off to sleep. Just because your eyes are closed doesn't mean that you won't derive any benefit from this. Have you ever slept while you sunbathed? You still got a suntan, didn't you? As for your ears, if you can learn a language from a tape recording running as you snore away, then I believe that your ears can receive a simple series of notes.

This is a wonderful tool for teachers to use to clear their

COLOR AND TONE

PURPLE
complete

RED
begin

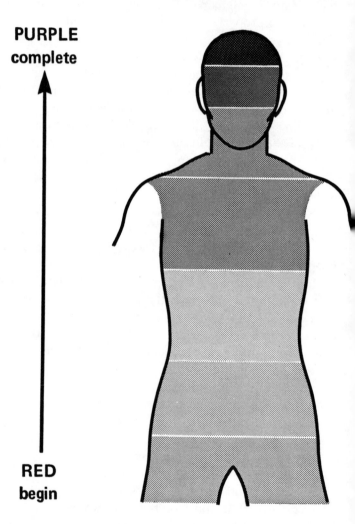

ATTUNEMENT SEQUENCE

TECHNIQUES

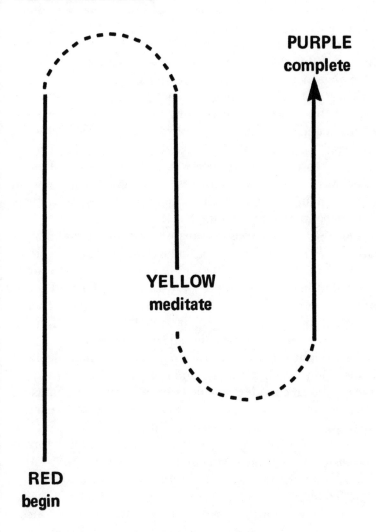

MEDITATION SEQUENCE

students before class (not to mention the teacher!). In fact, a fifth-grade teacher who is a client and student has been doing that every morning. Now the students practically beg for it. They say that it helps them settle down. They have noticed a distinct difference between themselves and the students in other classrooms who are not receiving this benefit.

Therapists are utilizing the soothing and balancing aspects of this process while treating their patients. If they use it beforehand to harmonize the physical body, it gives them a head start on treatment. Psychologists would find it a boon, I'm sure, to have their patients calmed down and tuned in before they saw them. (There *is* a danger that the patient might find, upon clearing out all those excess programs, there was no reason to have therapy.)

One doctor had the unfortunate experience of watching a patient die painfully over a period of two hours in the emergency room. He was so filled with her pain program afterwards that he could hardly cope with getting home. He ran through the colors twice at home, channeling their energy and vibration and released the terrible knots inside himself. He said afterwards that he believed it saved his sanity.

You might think of this as a psychic "vacuum cleaner" that is going to help round up and release all those other programs you are carrying around. I have found it useful as an extension of my own abilities when dealing with clients. There was a psychologist who had developed an allergy so painful that he could not bear to be touched. He had forced himself to be a physical person all his life, through positive displays and repressions, while actually he was a mental reactor. To manifest his repression and give his body an excuse to keep away from further damaging discord, he produced this allergy. Although we had spoken briefly in the counseling room, I decided to run the colors and tones with him first. This pinpointed the problem quickly. When the red flashed on the screen, he experienced acute discomfort. That helped convince both of us that there was more to the physical side of his life than he was in touch with.

For most of you, this is a very subtle process, and it will take time to recognize everything. You will find, as you become more attuned, that you feel good on some levels and uncomfortable on others. Become aware of these reactions because they are giving you an indication of where an imbalance is occurring. If you understand translation, you know that the next step is to identify what may be causing this and release it. These are very subtle feelings, but you will receive them clearer all the time. They are valuable feedback on what you are doing to your body.

Relax, meditate, or simply tune up your body—whatever particular need you have. Best of all, do all of them. Do them faithfully! As in any natural preventive or cure, it may take a while and you must be constant in your practice. This is not a drug which masks your imbalances, but a tool which may help correct them. I know that this, coupled with greater awareness of what you are doing to yourself, can mean you will never have to look any further than your own mirror for a psychic. And that is straight from the psychic's mouth!

TWELVE
Practical Exercises

If you have turned to this chapter before reading the preceding ones, STOP. These exercises are not intended to be casual little games, but to help you to develop keen psychic sensitivity. It is of no value, and could conceivably be harmful to you, to play around with them if you lack understanding of how your psychic mechanism works, and of the importance of balance and harmony among your centers.

Assuming that you have been with me all the way, it is time to put your awareness to some simple tests. Before you begin, it is always a good idea to run through the attunement sequence of colors from red to purple and get yourself well centered. Always practice on things that are a natural part of your life. It is pretty silly to practice psyching the stock market unless you are a broker or are planning to buy some stock. Start with things you know, things that are simple and free of emotional significance.

THE DAY'S EVENTS

In the morning, take a few minutes to look toward the day ahead. You may have a business meeting scheduled, or an appointment with a prospective customer or client. Will the event begin promptly, or will someone be late? How many people will be there? Men or women? How long will the meeting last? Will the outcome please you?

Perhaps you are going to meet a friend for lunch. Look in your mind's eye to see what she is wearing: Skirt or pants? Color? Fabric? Is she wearing a coat or sweater? Decide what sort of mood she will be in. Which of you will arrive first?

Psych your mail. How many pieces of mail will you get today? What type—business, personal or junk? Something expected or unexpected? Before you open a letter, see if you can feel its mood and content.

Many people have had the experience of answering the phone and saying, "I knew it was you." Make it a habit to decide, before picking up the phone, whether it is a man or a woman, a business or personal call, happy or unhappy in tone. You can get a lot of practice out of just one telephone call.

Notice that I suggest you go at this step by step. At first you may not be able to describe the appearance of the person you will meet later in the day, but you may be able to say whether it is a man or a woman. You may not know from whom a letter will come, but you see that you will receive a personal letter from someone. As time goes on and you continue to practice, more and more information will come to you. Chances are that you have been "knowing" things all along, but didn't pay any attention to it.

CHILDREN

Children like to play guessing games, probably because they are so intuitive. If you want to check out a child's psychic talent, do it with something simple and familiar. I used to work with my children using color. I would say, "I'm thinking of a color. What is it?" and have them tell me what color vibration they could feel. I used numbers in the same way. There is no need to go out and buy complicated things with which to practice. Simplicity is best.

PLAYING CARDS

You can get a lot of mileage out of playing cards. There are different vibrations for black and red; you can also learn to feel the amount of color on each card, and the higher and lower numbers. When I am working with a class, I usually start by having people differentiate between red and black. This means that they must find out how red and black feel to *them*. On a conscious level, colors seem the same to everyone. On an unconscious level, however, a color may excite some and irritate others, according to the meaning they have come to attach to it.

I discovered this when I first started teaching. I assumed that red would be the same to everyone—that is, bright and exciting. Black, I thought, was somber, sophisticated, or depressing. Then one day I was running cards with a psychologist, and her responses were 100 percent wrong. I couldn't understand this, as she was sensitive and should have gotten at least a couple right. Finally I asked her to describe how red and black felt to her, and found she had precisely the opposite feelings from mine. Now I have students verbalize the colors before we begin.

COLOR TESTS

Think of each of the seven colors that relate to our centers, and learn how each one feels to you. I don't mean by this how you react to it, but how it feels consciously. Then get someone to test you as I test my students. I try to have them respond through the part of the body to which the color corresponds: "I feel a tug at my heart, so it must be green," and so on.

I have talked about how people operate from one color more than from the others. In my classes, we try to visualize what someone's natural color is (their aura), and whether they are using it positively or whether some factor in their life has changed it. Is that a blue person, but working from green today? What does that tell you about his life? Don't strain your eyes looking for the physical manifestation of that color—it is more in the nature of mental imagery. The more you develop, the more solid it will appear, but you will still be seeing it with the mind's eye.

BUSINESS

If you are in business, decide before you sign a contract or approve a plan what your feelings are about it, and make notes. After the outcome is clear, review your notes. Try to do this on fairly short-term projects. After a few contracts, or whatever, you will learn the difference in feeling between a good deal and a bad one, and will start to pay more attention to that. Do the same thing when you hire a new employee. Make notes on how the person felt to you and what your expectations were. Then check it out some time later and see how accurate you were.

DRIVING YOUR CAR

I never stop practicing. When I get into my car to go somewhere, I psych whether I will get a parking place on the street or whether I will have to use a parking lot. I know one woman who says that parking places smell like Grand Marnier souffle to her! She can smell them before she can see them. Try deciding where you want to park and mentally clearing the space before you get there. Sometimes I am surprised to find no parking place, only to have someone pull out immediately. That counts, too.

On the freeway, I know whether I am going to see a police car. Police cars have entirely different vibrations, partly due to their equipment. They also carry heavy negative feelings that are attached to them by the public and by the traumatic incidents in which they are often involved. The friend I mentioned a moment ago says that police cars smell to her like Limburger cheese. There may be some truth to that old saying that (psychic) ignorance is bliss!

The only time I fail to sense police cars is when I ignore my intuition. Once, on my way to the doctor's office in Virginia Beach, every car on the road looked like a police car until I caught up with it, or it passed me. I thought I must be going crazy—they were all ordinary cars. But on the way home I was preoccupied with what the doctor had said, and exceeded the speed limit. It was dubious satisfaction to have my psychic ability verified when I was pulled over by a police car.

PERSONAL IDENTIFICATION TEST

This test is a bit more demanding, and it can help you to sharpen your skills quite a lot. Take turns doing it with a friend. Write the following data on a piece of paper:

1. Someone's name
2. Approximate age
3. Height, weight
4. Hair and eye colors
5. Marital status
6. Children (number, sex, ages)
7. Pets (number and type)
8. Strong personality traits
9. Strong likes and dislikes
10. Occupation

Fold the paper over to conceal the information and give it to your friend. Have her tell you as much as possible about the person you have chosen. Then reverse, and have her make the list and you do the psyching. The whole point of the exercise is to try to get an accurate feeling for the person who is the subject.

When I do this with you for the first time, I will walk you through it a step at a time. Is the person male or female? You'd be surprised how few people can differentiate between a male or female vibration when they first try. It's something so taken for granted that you may not be accustomed to recognizing the vibration. Once you get clear on how to identify the sex vibration, then it is time to hear the name. I will tell the first name, or both if the person is not known to you.

Now I want you to tell me how old the person is. Is he older than you? About the same age? Younger? A child?

There are a number of ways to get height. You can measure him against yourself, as you did with age. Do you have to look up to him, or down, or right in the eyes? Or you can take your hands and reach out to the person: Are you reaching up, down or straight across? With weight you can use your hands again. Is the person bony, well-muscled, soft? Another way to get his size is to mentally put certain sizes of clothing on him. Try a size 32 belt. Too small? Try a 34. Keep going until you feel that the belt fits perfectly. Try various trouser lengths until one feels right. Try on various shirt or jacket sizes until one fits. Do this until you *sense* that everything is the right size. (This works equally well for women.)

To get hair color, it sometimes works to shut your eyes and then open them suddenly to "look" at that person. Is the hair dark or light? Somewhere in between? With eyes, you can do the same thing, or you can (mentally) have him shut his eyes and then open them suddenly. Another idea is to picture the person with all features but eyes, then put a pair of blue ones in there. No? try brown. Keep experimenting until the color looks right. You see, this is not controlling you, you are in control. You can deliberately make your own composite until you are certain that everything is accurate.

At each stage of this process, I always ask you to tell me why you said each thing. It is important to know what you are basing decisions upon, so that you can rely on the cues that work best for you. I have you do this aloud so that you also *hear* how you are making your decisions. If you have said "dark hair" when it is blond, I want you to remember what it felt like to decide that. I will recap, "This is what you said. Does that always mean dark hair to you? Or can we, perhaps, see something there that may have pointed to light hair?" I want to take this apart for the beginner and put it. back together, so that the next time you will know how it felt when you were right.

You may wonder whether to go with your very first reaction, or to take your time making the decision. This varies from person to person. Some people are very accurate with first impressions. Others work best by thinking it out, being methodical, visualizing the alternatives. A person in one of my seminars said that his first impression comes very quickly, then in a few moments he gets a second one, and that is the correct one. In this case the conscious mind was throwing one in very fast, but a short time later the unconscious, true choice surfaced. You have to learn which way you work the best.

If you want to know if the person is married, visualize him and place a woman by his side. Does the figure of the woman get pushed away, or does it stay? In these days of people living together who are not married, you can put a wedding ring on the spouse's finger and see if it fits. Keep at it until you have a strong feeling of yes or no.

Try children. Put one in the picture and see if it stays. Add one at a time until you have one too many. See if you can place a boy there, or a girl. How old are they? Each refinement is something new to learn.

You are best at making your own rules and regulations as to how you get the information. You can incorporate your own experience and symbols that are significant to you. This is intensely personal. No one can tell you precisely what to do, because what it means to you is all that counts.

Pictures and Objects

Hold in your hands the picture of someone you don't know, and see how much you can get. Make notes and check them out, or do it with a friend who knows the person in the picture. This works well with inanimate objects that belong to someone else, because they give off vibrations too.

I have six favorite gold bracelets, each slightly different and each from a different giver. They all belong to me and are all of the same material: Why shouldn't they feel the same? But they don't. They were given to me by different people at different times and I have varying feelings about them. Through practice, you could tell me which was my absolute favorite, which giver I was most fond of, and whether the givers were friends, lovers or family. Objects retain all sorts of interesting vibrations.

Use All Your Senses

Don't overlook the five physical senses while you are developing your psychic awareness. Some people develop inner hearing so strongly that it seems it must be audible to everyone. My children, as well as some of my students, have heard my voice when I was not around. My youngest son used to run home from blocks away, certain he had heard me call him.

My housekeeper in Virginia Beach finally told me to stop calling her name after she got home. I said I didn't do that, but she insisted that I did—"just as clear as anything." One day while she was working upstairs I was on the first floor and saw a cobweb. I thought to myself, "I wish Charlie Mae would get that." No sooner had I thought it than she came downstairs saying, "I'm here, I'm here! You don't have to do that to me." She was evidently very psychic and we were attuned to one another. Don't expect to hear that clearly in the beginning.

Although we work with all five senses, sight, hearing and feeling are the more usual ones in psychic reception. Taste and smell come more slowly, unless there is deliberate practice of them. Once I sensed the acrid smell of cigar smoke while counseling, followed by the pungent stench of burning rubber tires. The cigar belonged to the deceased father of the client. The tires, however, presaged a car accident which occurred shortly after the appointment.

My students and I practice visualization over the telephone and in our houses at prearranged times. I ask them to tell me what I am doing at that hour, what I am wearing, and so on. I recall one woman, who was a high receiver, tapping in on me after an extremely busy day while I was dashing to prepare for dinner guests. I remember rushing about the kitchen saying, "Don't bother me now, I can't stop to work with you." The woman said later that she had been aware that I was very impatient that evening, though she didn't know why. I explained to her that she was quite accurate, and that her vibrations had simply been getting in my way.

DISTANCE TRAINING

The people at Stanford Research Institute in Menlo Park, California, have conducted some interesting tests to find out the distances at which ESP can work. They kept one person in a room while his partner went outside to a car where he opened a sealed envelope telling him to go to a designated location. The person who stayed in the room was then asked to describe as much as he could about the place where his partner had gone.

You will find their book *Mind-Reach** an interesting one to add to your library. It may inspire you to devise some of your own tests.

INSTANT FEEDBACK

All these exercises are designed to help you develop your accuracy, so always choose things that you can prove immediately. It won't be much help to predict an event months or even years ahead while you are still learning the ropes. Form the habit of looking ahead a few moments or hours and seeing what will happen. When you find you have been right, it will be a big boost to your confidence. Think up your own exercises where the answers are immediate, and keep score on your accuracy. You may be amazed how quickly you progress.

GOING OUT ON A LIMB

The men in my Santa Barbara law enforcement seminar told me their biggest handicap at the beginning was fear of being wrong. I think this is true for everyone. That initial feeling of going out on a limb is one we tend to find very uncomfortable, especially when we are in the presence of others.

It is very important for you to know that everything you get has meaning. If it seems to be wrong, that is only because you are not yet expert at translating. For instance, suppose you were doing a personal identification test and you said that the subject was five feet tall. Your partner corrected

---

Mind-Reach: Scientists Look at Psychic Ability, by Russell Targ and Harold Puthoff. (New York: Dell Publishing Company, 1977.)

you, pointing out that the person is actually 5'10". You may have been picking up that the subject always wanted to be tall. Or that her father was tall. Go back and look at the impression again to see if you can place the bit of information correctly. Remember the case of the woman who asked if her brother-in-law would return safely from Vietnam; the mid-air crash I saw was totally unrelated to that case, and only careful reviewing of all the received data showed me that. But there *was* a mid-air crash. Your reception is never right or wrong. You simply need to gain experience in translating what you get.

There will be different levels and degrees of accuracy as you go along. Don't expect miracles right away. In some ways it is like becoming a wine taster. The first times you sip wine you aren't going to be able to say which grape, which year, or where grown. The wine taster perfects her ability as her palate becomes educated. It is the same with the psychic sense. If you really want to make your life more understandable and easier to handle, you must practice, practice, practice.

CLASSES

It's fun to practice with others, and to have someone a little more advanced (experienced) help you take the first few steps. That is why people take classes. But it need not be a lengthy or expensive affair. Many courses run as long as a year, or two. Mine is eight weeks long. I give my students the basics and they can take this knowledge and practice at their own speed. You don't stay in driver education very long; they take you out on the road, teach you the basics, and the rest is up to you. That is how I see the development of the psychic.

Some students are so accustomed to teachers from childhood demanding things of them that they are perturbed when I don't cram it down their throats. I tell them that I can't make them practice—that if they want to achieve this capability it becomes their responsibility to themselves to do so. I will break down into understandable language what transpires, and how. The rest is up to them.

You are the only one who can make the decision about whether you really want and need to get in touch with your innermost self. I have provided the tools. I hope you will enjoy using them, and that very shortly the psychic in your life is you.

THIRTEEN
Psychic Etiquette

At the beginning of humankind, everybody had ESP and took it for granted. They needed it for survival. It told them where the food was, when to take shelter, and what was lurking in the dark. As these early people began to band together in groups, they divided up the jobs. By this time they had realized, as I have, that this psychic stuff takes time and work. So they appointed somebody in the group to do it for them. Over thousands of years people forgot that everybody could do it. Eventually those charged with the psychic work of their communities began to realize that they had enormous power, so they surrounded their tasks with a great deal of mystery and ritual and became adept at the manipulation of heavy symbolism in order to impress their people. They, too, had forgotten that they were just like everyone else.

Unfortunately this is true of many psychics today. They have come to believe their own "publicity," and there are still plenty of them left in the lightning-bolt school of thought. These are the ones who speak of the "gift" or the "power" with which they have been endowed, and who insist that they in no way control what comes to them psychically. A lot of harm has been done by such irresponsible attitudes.

One particularly destructive manifestation of this is the psychic who is willing to sit around and make predictions about famous people for publication in newspapers and magazines. This is a really loathesome invasion of privacy, and I could not be more opposed to it. The only conceivable reason for doing this is to make headlines. Meanwhile, those whose lives have been intimately invaded without their permission are left to make the best of it. It is absolutely unethical to enter another person's consciousness without being asked to do so.

There are currently some prominent psychics who have set themselves up as Superman or Superwoman to the world. One of these maintains a headquarters staff to support the many activities in which the psychic is involved. While on the road, this psychic will telephone the staff to ask them to do some of the psyching and predicting for the next scheduled appearance. Here the work of perhaps a dozen people is being put forth as that of one. I have told a member of that staff I feel they are perpetuating a fraud. This famous psychic is being made to look superhuman. Apart from the dishonesty involved, the public is being shortchanged into believing that only one in a million could possibly be so "gifted." Poppycock. There are lots of anonymous workers behind that facade.

Because of all the mumbo jumbo that has come to be associated with psychic phenomena, I have found that many genuine psychics feel pressured to make a sensation, and some of them resort to trickery and even downright fraud. When I lived in Virginia, the local spiritualist church appointed a new minister who was a gifted medium.

Evidently he didn't feel he was spectacular enough, so he resorted to sessions in which objects would fly through the air and spirits of loved ones would appear in draperies. He was constantly telling the people at these sessions that they must not try to touch the spirits that appeared. I became very sure that there was something or someone very solid beneath all the floating fabric. Finally, the minister went on a long vacation. During that time, a member of the congregation had to enter the man's house to find something belonging to the church. Instead, he found a large box of stones and gems that had frequently flown through the air as apports (materializations from the spirit world). A collection of spirit draperies also "materialized." The minister's vacation became permanent.

I deeply resent this sort of shenanigans, because it makes genuine psychic work so much more difficult for the rest of us. It is a great waste of my energy and time if I am expected to establish my credibility each time I enter a case or counsel a client. I won't do it anymore; there is too much important work to be done, and my work speaks for itself.

You have every right to expect very high quality from a psychic counselor, and you should demand it. The psychic consultation should be like any other transaction, in that you get value for your money. We have all been led to be in awe of the "power," and who are we to criticize what we get? Well, we have every right to interrupt a vague monologue, pay off the person for the time spent, and leave.

If I were to go to a psychic and ask to be told about my mother's health, knowing she is in very grave condition, and hear, "I'm not allowed to see that," I'd say, "But that's why I came here. *Who* doesn't allow you to see that?"

If I ask, "Am I going to get married again?" and hear, "Let's talk about your soul progression," I am going to get up and go home. If the psychic is not willing to take a stand on something that can be proven, don't bother with him.

Some psychics may let their life experiences color their readings. One card reader was paralyzed and confined to his home. I noticed that his bitterness over his fate often seeped into his readings, making them very pessimistic. A woman psychic who had been the neglected daughter of an alcoholic father lost all perspective when any mention of what she regarded as "demon rum" came into the picture. This is completely unprofessional.

As a psychic, you must filter your own experience out of the situation with a client. You do this by being aware of yourself and how you see the world, and detaching from that. All of us have had experiences which could be allowed to remain heavy, but I really try to work through mine as I go along so that I am not wrestling with something that may color my work. I have also learned to go beyond programs to the being level when I am with a client. It is a matter of self-training, which any self-respecting psychic will have done.

In my counseling sessions, I am always very specific and I expect you to ask questions. I will not only tell you about a tall-dark-stranger-with-a-lot-of-money, but I will also tell you where this man is coming from, what he's done in the past, what he's doing now, and what the two of you have in store if you choose to marry. I will tell you the reasons you are likely to marry and what vibrations are interacting to make this happen. I, and others like me, will give you information in a format that you can take away and use. I will hope to increase your understanding of yourself.

If you are in the midst of a crisis, I will tell you what patterns in the past have set you up for it, what are some probable outcomes, and how to prepare for them. I will tell you how to avoid a crisis if there is a better course. If you are someone in need of this kind of counseling, you won't get much satisfaction from a few vague and disconnected generalizations.

Quite apart from charlatans or frauds, there are many psychics who believe, in all innocence, that they have certain restrictions—that they can only operate in a certain way or on a particular level. Perhaps their religious beliefs exclude such things as reincarnation or prophecy, and they limit themselves accordingly. Others will insist that only God can do the work through the lightning bolt of inspiration. I have heard psychics say, "I can't give you that sort of information," or, "I can't read you without asking permission of my guides," or, "I never see material things, so I can't tell you whether you will have money or not." This is not strictly true. They *could* tell you about your finances, or divorce, or death, but since they have programmed themselves not to (because they don't wish to see such things), they won't. There are invalids who have convinced themselves that they cannot walk, so they cannot. If I go to someone who says he has to go through a ritual first, fine. I just watch him go through it. But I know that it is an arbitrary way of warming up and isn't strictly necessary.

Some psychics say they can only prophesy during a full moon, or under some other conditions. If they trained themselves, they could see just as well under all phases of the moon. Any time our glands are stimulated, we are going to be more open to an altered state of consciousness. If we look at what makes our glands work, then we can take proper care of them. People no longer need cling to the old explanations of mysterious, uncontrollable forces granted to only a special few.

Many of the old-school psychics never meant to fool anyone; they just did not understand their abilities themselves. If once they made an accurate prediction during a full moon, then they assumed that it was at full moon they would always be correct. If information came in a flash sometimes, and other times not at all, they naturally assumed the nature of their awareness to be unpredictable, or that only God could determine when to allow it. These people perpetuated ignorance *unintentionally* because they really didn't know the answers.

The trained ability of the psychic—and I wish to emphasize *trained*—can be used like a pencil. You can make an X with it, you can sign your name, write a novel, compose a concerto or write a letter. You can even draw a picture. Once you have learned to use it, you can use it any way you wish. All knowledge is there for the taking. I am doing something that I was willing to take the time to learn and practice. Because of that, I can do it a lot better than the person who is waiting for the bolt out of the blue.

Responsibility is a theme that necessarily runs through all of my work. I have certain responsibilities to my clients that I take very seriously. I have already talked about my responsibility to give adequate, concrete information in a way that you can easily understand. Just as important is that I help you to help yourself. I will have done you no service if you become dependent on me to lead you through life a step at a time. It is my responsibility to provide you with good counsel for the immediate problem plus the insight and knowledge to handle similar circumstances later on.

My attitude toward doing healings is closely related to this. I define illness as an imbalance in the physical mechanism that is brought about by negative programs. I feel that the psychic does you no favor just to lay on hands and effect a cure. The negative programs will still exist, and are likely to manifest in another way. I prefer to work with the client in weeding out the negative programs and refer him to an excellent medical practitioner for treatment of the illness itself.

I also have certain responsibilities to myself. An important one is to keep myself in balance by remembering to release information and negative energy. When I am working with a client, she has my undivided attention and I have her "file" in my head. When I am finished, I release it. I very seldom recall what I have said, unless I deliberately take time to do so. If she comes for another session, I'll open the file and have another look, but I don't waste storage space by keeping it in my conscious mind.

It is very important for all counselors, psychic or otherwise, to use this release process. It involves letting the energy flow from the solar plexus up to the head for interpretation and then letting it go. If you don't do this, a bottleneck of programs will occur in the yellow center, and sooner or later the stoppage causes damage emotionally, physically, mentally, or all three. It is an occupational hazard to leave files hanging around inside of you. Put them away each time you finish with them.

People are full of misconceptions about psychics. A prevalent one is that we are constantly reading everyone's mind. Not only would this be an invasion of privacy, but I make it part of my responsibility to myself to work only when I am on a case or with a client. At a party, the last thing I want to do is work! Often a stranger will approach me saying, "What do you see about me?" I generally respond with something like, "You look like you have good taste in clothes."

Another responsibility I have to myself is to charge a fee commensurate with the value of my service. I had to wade through the money problem. Remember the psychic long ago who advised me always to charge a fee. She told me, "In the Bible it says that the laborer is worthy of his hire. You will have a hard time remembering that."

When I was still vacillating about how to value my time, an incident occurred that helped me to come to a decision. One day a woman flew all the way from New York to Virginia Beach to consult me. I spent the hour she had scheduled plus an additional hour with her and felt it had been a good session. At the end she asked what the fee was. "Why don't you give me what you like," I said. She handed me five dollars and left. I laughed and laughed because I realized that I had been taught a good lesson. If she had been generous, I might have followed that procedure for the rest of my life. But her miserly response brought home to me that I was responsible for placing value on myself.

Money has always been surrounded with confusion by my profession. There has been a misconception that any mixture of the psychic and money taints the "powers" involved. (This, of course, goes back to the misconception that there are any mysterious "powers" to begin with. You know by now that psychic awareness is a natural attribute.) It is as absurd to contend that psychics will lose their awareness because they charge fees as to hold that a singer will lose his voice if he is paid for performing. As with every other human being, the psychic is responsible for taking care of his own needs and those of his family. If he doesn't charge enough to satisfy his own needs and desires, how can he be free to help anyone else with theirs.

People sometimes call and want me to work free of charge. Usually they say they have no money. Now I say, "I certainly understand. When you do feel you can afford it, please call me and I'll be glad to give you an appointment." I do some counselings free, but I like to feel that I have the right to make that decision myself. Occasionally a person will want to barter for my services. I find money to be far more useful, and so I ask them to exchange some of their time for money before we make an appointment.

You see, each partner in the client-psychic transaction has a responsibility to it. Here is another example. One time I let myself be talked into going to the office on a Saturday, though I have made it a rule not to work on weekends. The woman who called begged me to see her, saying it was an emergency. Finally I consented. I raced through the weekly chores and errands of a busy Saturday to be punctual for the one o'clock appointment. The woman kept me waiting until three. She had been unable to leave a shopping excursion with a friend, she said. Another lesson learned, I refused to see her at that hour. I now know that it is part of good service to my clients to be businesslike. It implies that we value each other equally and that we are willing to be responsible to each other.

People who are new to the world of ESP occasionally come to me feeling rather skeptical. Sometimes they want to know if I am 100 percent accurate. "Are *you* 100 percent accurate in your work?" I ask. Or they want to know if I've ever been wrong. "Have *you* ever been wrong?" I wonder. The only thing I can guarantee is that I will continue to grow in my field, with more practice and more experience as time goes by, and that they will get everything that hard work and study have brought me. That is what I can promise, no more and no less.

I see no reason that a psychic should try to look larger than life. When I see those who make national names for themselves by trying to appear superhuman, it makes me very angry. Are they so insecure that they can never be seen to make a mistake? There has always been a certain tendency in this field to blame mistakes on something outside: the cards, the guides, the crystal ball. I suppose it is only natural to use these crutches in the beginning, but as a professional you must take responsibility for your interpretations. Only then will you be able to serve your clients honorably and well.

Sometimes when I talk about the responsibilities of a professional psychic, particularly regarding invasion of privacy, someone will ask about the possibility of mind control. Of course it is possible, though it may often be unintentional. If I can undergo surgery for pains that turn out to be someone else's, or reach for an aspirin bottle when someone else has a migraine, then I am picking up other people's programs and confusing them with my own. The same thing is true if I look at a menu and feel confused because I'm picking up other people's choices. The other people are controlling my mind to some extent. The appropriate defense against this is precisely the same as that against intentional mind control.

The only way any person or any foreign power can control our minds is if we do not understand how it happens. The remedy is to "know thyself." When we have taken the trouble to know ourselves thoroughly we will notice when changes come and other people's thought forms are dominating us, and we can bring ourselves back on course. Otherwise we can get caught up in playing out others' programs. Knowledge is going to illuminate this whole area of human consciousness.

I find it intriguing to look to the future and speculate on

the kind of world it will be when each individual has recognized his own psychic potential completely. There will be no possibility of one nation's secretly planning to attack another, because the other will know about it instantly. On a personal level, lovers or married people would be able to conceal neither their true feelings nor their infidelities from one another, so a bad relationship will resolve itself much faster without years of game-playing. One would never try to put something over on somebody, because they would know. Everything would be out in the open, and we would have a world of truth.

Obviously if this were to happen all at once it would be so cataclysmic that we would no doubt be like the people of Belfast and need psychiatrists to help us deal with the change. But if it comes gradually, so that eventually babies are born into a world where truth is the norm, it could be wonderful.

People who today are training themselves in psychic awareness are in the vanguard. They know that ignorance, both of professionals and of the public, has been the only hindrance to full development of this human capability. If you have decided to be part of the vanguard, you have probably already started working on the practical exercises and tuning your psychic radio through good nutrition and meditative balancing.

At the beginning, students always want to know when it will be safe to rely on their ESP, and when to be cautious. Well, psychic sense is a tool, and first you must learn to use it. If you do the sort of exercises that give instant feedback, you will have a good yardstick of your accuracy. Begin with rather superficial things and move at your own pace into areas that are more significant to you. Trust yourself to know how reliable you are. At some point you will find that your answer on something is so unexpectedly accurate that you are absolutely amazed. So my favorite advice is this: When you learn to amaze yourself, go right ahead and do it!